Minding What Matters

Minding What Matters

PSYCHOTHERAPY AND THE
BUDDHA WITHIN

by Robert Langan

foreword by Robert Coles

WISDOM PUBLICATIONS • BOSTON

Wisdom Publications, Inc.
199 Elm Street, Somerville MA 02144 USA
www.wisdompubs.org

Library of Congress Cataloging-in-Publication Data

Langan, Robert.
  Minding what matters : psychotherapy and the Buddha within / by Robert Langan.
    p. cm.
  Includes index.
  ISBN 0-86171-353-2 (pbk. : alk. paper)
  1. Buddhism and psychoanalysis. 2. Psychotherapy—Religious aspects—Buddhism.
  3. Buddhism—Psychology. I. Title.
  BQ4570.P755L36 2006
  294.3'36150195—dc22

                          2005037920

"Cambridge," translated by Hoyt Rogers, copyright © 1999 by Maria Kodama; translation copyright (c) 1999 by Hoyt Rogers, from SELECTED POEMS by Jorge Luis Borges, edited by Alexander Coleman. Used by permission of Viking Penguin, a division of Penguin Group (USA) Inc

Excerpt from THE SNOW LEOPARD by Peter Matthiessen, copyright © 1978 by Peter Matthiessen. Used by permission of Viking Penguin, a division of Penguin Group (USA) Inc.

"Keeping Things Whole" and "Jessica, My Daughter" from SELECTED POEMS by Mark Strand, copyright © 1979, 1980 by Mark Strand. Used by permission of Alfred A. Knopf, a divison of Random House, Inc.

"Free and Easy: A Spontaneous Vajra Song" in N. Khenpo, ed. (S. Das, trans.) Natural Great Perfection: Dzogchen Teaching and Vajra Songs (Ithaca: Snow Lion, 1995). Reprinted by permission.

ISBN 0-86171-353-2
10 09 08 07 06
5 4 3 2 1

Cover design by Laura Shaw • Interior by Gopa & Ted2, Inc. • Set in Perpetua 12.5/15.

Wisdom Publications' books are printed on acid-free paper and meet the guidelines for permanence and durability of the Production Guidelines for Book Longevity set by the Council on Library Resources.

Printed in the United States of America

This book was produced with environmental mindfulness. We have elected to print this title on 50% PCW recycled paper. As a result, we have saved the following resources: 24 trees, 17 million BTUs of energy, 2.140 lbs. of greenhouse gases, 8,881 gallons of water, and 1,141 lbs. of solid waste. For more information, please visit our web site, www.wisdompubs.org

Learn where is wisdom, where is strength, where is understanding,
That thou mayest also know length of days and life,
The source of the light in the eyes and peace.
—JAMES WALKER* (1794–1874)
Inscription on memorial bust,
Cambridge, Massachusetts

. . . As in dreams
behind high doors there is nothing,
not even emptiness.
As in dreams,
behind the face that looks at us there is no one.
Obverse without a reverse,
one-sided coin, the side of things.
That pittance is the boon
tossed to us by hastening time.
We are our memory,
we are that chimerical museum of shifting shapes,
that pile of broken mirrors.
—JORGE LUIS BORGES*
"Cambridge" (1969)

TABLE OF CONTENTS

FOREWORD

WHAT FOLLOWS in this book is a large gift of inwardness that becomes a personal, professional, social, cultural, and spiritual reflection. Robert Langan wants to understand who he is, who he has become, and who we, his readers, may come to be. His inward desire becomes our gift. Through meeting him and his thoughts and ideas, his clinical work, his philosophical approach to life, his moral and psychoanalytic self-scrutiny that more than matches the intense psychological self-questioning of his profession, we become his colleagues, even compatriots. We are fellow seekers who want to use our minds and hearts and souls the better to fulfill our humanity. Determined awareness, fearlessly pursued, can become a manner of being that gives us some leeway over the rush of reflexes, impulses, and memories that awaits us around any corner of our lived experience. Determined awareness can open a way through time, circumstance, and possibility.

These wonderfully literate, compelling, knowing pages summon the reader to wonder about life's whys and wherefores, its purposes and meanings. As I read them, I was reminded of the words of Erik Erikson, a child psychoanalyst, an author, and a teacher of mine as well: "In India [while preparing to write *Gandhi's Truth*] I thought of Buddhism, its effort to explore consciousness, to discover what makes each of us the individuals we have turned out to be. There's where Freud meets, in the long run of time, the Buddha. We are among those who keep trying to find his truths, to savor them. When we practice psychoanalysis, sitting there, doing that clinical work, we are yearning, as Freud yearned, for human truths, for a wisdom that ends our pain, for a self-knowledge that helps us walk unfettered." Although Erikson was quick thereafter to declare himself "unaware of Buddhist principles," in his moment of introspective connection he saw in Buddha and Freud two wise observers of their fellow human beings, two thinkers able to help others be more candidly self-aware, more bravely willing to recognize how we can lose ourselves to blind passion become a ruling force of our day-to-day lives.

For Langan, the challenge to discover what makes us who we are is a vigorously demanding one. It is the clearheaded, sensitive, and carefully informed pursuit of this life's significance, the effort to find what and who we are and to what purpose during our time spent here. This pursuit encompasses the looking inward of philosophy and theology, and as well, the looking outward toward others. When a clinician reflects a particular person's words and ways of being and doing, that knowledge from without can become within the patient a boost toward self-understanding.

The Buddha concentrated mightily on the reality of human being, and Freud likewise. Their light informs Langan's shining, even entrancing vision of what it is possible to do and to be, for a clinician, a patient, for a friend, a relative, a mate—indeed, for any of us in relation to one another. We may each catch sight of the others around us with a certain respect that becomes reverential in nature.

Robert Coles, M.D.
Concord, Mass.

Preface

BOTH BUDDHISM AND PSYCHOANALYSIS encourage turning attention to the mind itself. Cultivating attention, minding the mind, indeed, mending the mind, though understood differently by the two practices, are strategies similarly contrived to ease human suffering. I am a practitioner, inevitably in my own evolving way, of both Buddhism and psychoanalysis. What have I in mind that you might mind as well?

I have in mind an excursion to places odd and curious. These places exist only in mind—in our mind, to the extent that we go there together. We go into constellations of memories, associations, latitudes of reality, longitudes of time. My hope is that I, in the writing of these places, and you, in the reading, might be carried along by the flow of words not just to the passing scenery the words describe, but to an awareness of the flow itself; not just to objects of attention, but to the turnings of attention itself.

Accordingly, this book has a peculiar structure, like a double helix perpetually turning from one sort of writing to another. The two strands of writing intertwine in an effort to draw attention to how one engages with what is written, how one falls into a relationship with the patterns of words. The one strand is of essays musing on topics relevant to Buddhism and psychoanalysis; these alternate with fictional vignettes describing an imaginary psychoanalytic case, the second strand. The essays, ironically, invite an analytic assessment of the thinking they contain, while the vignettes of an analysis invite a willingness unanalytically to hear a story, to go with the flow.

Buddhism and psychoanalysis are in the foreground of the essays, but in the unspoken background of the vignettes. Going from the one sort of writing to the other entails turning attention, noticing the disjunction. When the one sort of attention turns to the other you may notice, as I do in the writing, a space between. The book is peculiar because it is full of holes. What is missing matters, not because it must be found, but because being gone it shapes what's here.

The holes are part of a curving lattice: concerns touched on in the essays show up in the vignettes, and vice versa. To my mind, a Buddhist sensibility is implicit in the flow of a psychoanalytic conversation, and a pychoanalytic sensibility implicit in Buddhism. Emptiness, remembering, time, death, virtue, happiness, dismay, hope, our mattering the one to the other—the book is about these human concerns, both in the abstract, as recurrent topics in the essays, and in subjective experience, in the dialogue of the vignettes.

The first chapter, "Attending Within," discusses the nature of introspective attention from the perspectives of Buddhism and of psychoanalysis. The first vignette, *"The Consulting Room,"* shows an interplay of psychoanalytic attention between analyst and analysand. By holding things in mind, attention creates and reifies the world. What is not held in mind is from one vantage the unconscious, from another vantage emptiness. The second chapter, "Finding Emptiness," adopts each vantage. In the vignette, *"Opening,"* our analysand finds, too, an emptiness before him. The chapters proceed, from "Consciousness" to "Mysteries Between" to "Attachments" to "Memories, Dreams, Perceptions"; themes recur; the vignettes intertwine. The intertwining sets up a counterpoint between the chapter essays and the fictional vignettes; it poses them in dialogue.

And who am I to treat such topics, to imagine such a dialogue? Like you, just like you, I find myself living my human life, thinking, feeling, minding a way in the world. We are sentient beings, born of and with one another, briefly alive together here now. Who are we not to treat such topics? Each of us holds a universe in mind.

Each of us holds in mind what others have told us. Occasionally throughout the text you will find an asterisk, which marks another crossover in the lattice. Please ignore it, until later. Later, consult the "Sources and Associations" to find who has come to mind, whose shadow shades the words. The section is not simply a compilation of footnotes, but a reflection on the formative context of others' words. As such, the section can be read in its own right as a didactic commentary on each chapter, grounding each chapter in the work of others. Finally, the "References" section, like a background bookshelf, leads further to others' words.

Each of us as well is linked to all of those who, wittingly or not, have taught and helped and influenced us. I want to acknowledge and thank, on the psychoanalytic side, Erik Erikson, who inspired my pursuit of a psychoanalysis whose "province is life"; and Robert Coles, who fostered my first undergraduate efforts in psychosocial writing; Bernie Kalinkowitz, who imbued clinical psychology with passion and joy; Robert R. Holt, who maintained rigor. My two analysts stay cloaked in confidentiality, except to me, who came to know myself through knowing them. Emmanuel Ghent acknowledged spirituality. Donnell Stern centralized the nature of experience. Stephen A. Mitchell vitalized a relational openness to ideas. Michael Eigen and Adam Phillips unshackled psychoanalytic writing. And through it all, Philip M. Bromberg has been mentor, listener, reader, kindly critic, and friend. These are a few of the many.

On the Buddhist side, I thank B.B.B. Shah Deva, whose welcoming acquaintance led to Nepal and my first brush with Tibetan Buddhism. Chögyam Trungpa Rinpoche brought Tibetan Buddhism to New York when I was susceptible to a naïve conversion; his not-so-crazy wisdom was for me to stay in school. Robert Thurman trumpeted Buddhism's relevance to our contemporary predicament. Kyabje Gelek Rinpoche and the Jewel Heart sangha made it personal.

Jack Engler, Joseph Goldstein, Larry Rosenberg, Ajahn Sucitto, Jeremy Safran, and, catalytically, Mark Epstein, have all reflected on psychology East and West. Their reflections dapple my thoughts. Josh Bartok, my editor at Wisdom Publications, helped me to try to free those thoughts. Their presences are orienting reminders to turn, once again, to the present. And Sara Weber is the axis on which so much turns.

How many names, yet how many more: parents and family, friends, lovers, colleagues, teachers and supervisors, supervisees and students, and always, in anything but anonymous relationship to me, my patients. Then there are others I know only through their written words. So many people, so many associations. Like you, I am touched by multitudes. From multitudes come I. Some are distant, some are dead, yet alive to memory, still interdependently present in mind. All of them, knowingly or not, are linked to this book. As, having read thus far, are you.*

1.

ATTENDING WITHIN

PEOPLE DO THINGS for different reasons, though sometimes their reasons are the same. Each of us is different, yet because we have our being different in common, we find ourselves the same. We are the same in our difference, while our differences are not the same.

We have in common the experience of living a life, each life different. We have in common our human being, so much the same.* Each of us faces the dilemma of how best to live that life encumbered, as it is, with inevitable sickness, suffering, and death. What do we do? We look to each other for answers.

Your answer cannot wholly be mine, for I am different. Nor can mine be yours, since we are not the same. And yet, methods we find of coming to answers may benefit us each in the same way.

One method is attending within—attending introspectively to how attention itself rises and falls, takes shape and dissolves in the ongoing stream of experience. "Entering the stream" is a description, as it happens, of following the meditative method of the Buddha. Likewise, "evenly hovering" attention to the ripples and eddies of thought and feeling, to the swirl of associations, marks the psychoanalytic method begun by Freud.*

The stream of the Buddha and the stream of psychoanalysis are, indeed, different, and yet with their differences in common, they may, at least strategically, be the same.

Once, years ago, near the end of my psychoanalytic training, I dreamt of a stream. I was in the mountains, stepping from stone to stone in the streambed of a rushing brook. The water loudly burbled and hissed. Then I heard, intermingled with the water's sound, a humming, a cheerful musical tune. It came from upstream, just ahead of me around a bend. I hurried to catch up with the singer who, when I rounded the bend, had already hurried ahead, past another turning. I thought I caught a glimpse of a monk's red robe. I hurried in pursuit, never catching up, smiling at the hide-and-seek joke played on me. Then I realized that the humming was coming from my own mouth.

I thought the monk was someone different. He and I were the same.

In this waking world I am no monk. How do I know? When I pause to reflect, I have no memory of vows, no recollection of years in a monastery; in fact, the years of my life are quite seamlessly accounted for. No one suggests otherwise. I hold firmly to the continuity of my life. I retain my ongoing familiarity with my life story and thereby myself. I know who I am.

Or do I? One, and then another, suggests otherwise: the Buddha, then Freud. They suggest not that my facts are wrong, but that my very understanding of facts is misguided. That my view has been partial their undermining suggestions agree: You are not who you think you are. You are more, and paradoxically, less. Both agree: You are more than the limitations of your thought, as attending within can reveal. The Buddha goes further: You are less, alas, than you might now wish, from which wish seeing what *is* can liberate you. You are neither confined, nor confinable, to your factitious self.

I found myself in the streambed of a rushing brook, formed myself in pursuit in a mountainous world, forming, formed in, formed of the rush of experience, its source always just ahead, unseeable, an emptiness before me.

His diligent practice of attending to the flow of experience within led the Buddha to acknowledge the existence of an ongoing self,* but to recognize that existence as ephemeral, impermanent, built on the shifting sands of altering circumstance. He found no bedrock, no intrinsic self. Still more radically, beyond the horizon of familiar assumption, he found neither self nor no-self.* The Buddha awakened, as if from a dream, to what is. What is lies beyond linguistic categorization, beyond concepts and their negations. The method to find what is requires reshaping one's life to follow in the footsteps of the Buddha, finding out, step by step, for oneself.

Step by steppingstone I hurried along that dreamtime streambed to discover, in another small way, I was not who I thought I was. Perhaps, just a little, I awakened. I awoke to remember the dream.

Freud's footsteps led him to dreams, and to the discovery that they hold clues as to what is. Yet Freud did not go so far as the Buddha. His early psychoanalytic method's modest aim was only to relieve neurotic suffering, not to alter one's fundamental way of being in the world. At best, the relief of neurotic suffering could leave the patient with the "common misery of mankind."* The insidious suggestion of psychoanalysis was that you are keeping secrets from yourself. What is, as revealed by psychoanalysis, includes those wishes, ragings, and lusts previously forbidden to conscious awareness. What is, is not a pretty picture. You are not who you think you are.

For example, let us say* the patient, a beautiful baroness, no longer young, climbs Freud's long flight of stairs for help with a mysterious ailment: She has been unable to move her hand since the day her father died. As instructed, she lies down on the analytic couch, lying languidly atop the kilim which covers it, the tresses of her hair spilling over a linen antimacassar, her limp hand at her side. Freud asks her questions. He tells her, insofar as she is able, to say whatever comes to mind, however seemingly relevant or irrelevant. Sessions pass, day after day. Together they notice her hesitations, her misgivings, her associations to her dreams, her feelings toward the famous doctor. Finally, they come to the realization that she was not simply the devoted daughter, constant at the side of her father's deathbed until he no longer needed her. She also had a wish, a wish nearly too unbearable to know. She had wished to pour his medicine, all of it, a lethal dose, into a midnight glass, and so to pay him back for his interference with the man she loved and his insistence that she marry instead the baron. Her writhing hand flies to her mouth, but cannot stifle the startled scream of recognition. She is no longer the innocent. What ailed our imaginary baroness was an attachment to a version of herself. Yet she is not the murderer she might have been. She may come to see herself as an injured party, or the victim of her own compliance, or the chin-held-high aristocrat who will not comply again. The implicit premise of psychoanalysis, in its early days, is that she is not who she thinks she is; its promise is that she can find out who she really is.

A century flickers by. Freud is dead; the generation of psychoanalysts who knew him is dead, replaced by another generation, and another. The premise of psychoanalysis remains the same: what is unconscious affects what is conscious. No longer the same is the promise of a definitive truth. You are not who you think you are, because "you" are a habit (or a collection of habits) of thought, a habitual turn of mind. There remains always more to discover about oneself; because there is always more, one is perpetually incomplete, forming while unforming. Psychoanalytic attention reveals this forming while unforming, this paradoxical unforming while forming, which "I" resist to stay the same, which "I" engage the better to choose differently.

Contemporary psychoanalysis* sustains the promise, or at least the hope, to free the patient from a too-stultifying version of self. But the promise does not end by replacing an illusory version with the real. Instead, version follows version, versions coëxist with versions, the real is evanescent, impermanent, a provisional circumstance contingent on shifting conditions. That "real" self is ever ungraspable, always (it seems) just ahead out of sight around the next turn in the stream of experience. Nonetheless, how one lives, how one chooses to shape experience, matters.

What really matters is how one increases, or diminishes, suffering, both knowingly and not. People come for psychoanalysis out of suffering. Their lives and circumstances and personalities differ, but their hope to live with diminished suffering is the same. Psychoanalytically speaking, the root of much suffering is inattention. Freud's goal of making the unconscious conscious entails noticing, perhaps for the first time, elements of experience, patterns of action, motivations and assumptions heretofore little attended. The expedient choices of childhood—as to what one must do in order to be good—can open to choice once again. With choice comes freedom. Being the unfree victim of one's life can be seen as a choice—and a poor choice. One is answerable* for choices, and their consequences in suffering. One is free to choose again, and otherwise. One can know better how to take responsibility for choosing. Yet choosing is less a matter of making rational decisions than it is a willing opening to the stream of experience. The suffering and the hurts of the past, having happened, do not change; what can change is what one can notice now, and thereby how one can choose to react to the past, present, and future.

The crux of psychoanalysis is the alteration of awareness through the method of attending within. Psychoanalysis provides a setting and a relationship in which to notice the play of attention, the turnings of the mind. Further, psychoanalysis takes as an object of attention the relationship between the two people in the consulting room, and the openness of that relationship to change. Psychoanalysis is an experiment of attention, an effort to notice what you notice and to begin to notice what you don't notice, what you (both of you in the consulting room) typically and habitually tend to overlook and leave out, or insist on leaving in. We look for interrelatedness in everything, in what gets talked about and what doesn't, in dreams, in the odd remark, the fleeting feeling. As we coast along, following thoughts, their storylines, their pictures of the world, our crucial analytic sidestep is at least on occasion to work free from the flow, to let go. We make the space to notice how we perpetuate more of the same—one thought does lead to another. In trepidation, we shy from opening to unknown difference. To open is the hard thing, to let go of clinging.

We may notice how our reactions to hurts of the past, our efforts to feel better, have become the habits of the present we assiduously perpetuate to ensure more of the same for the future. The hurts of the past recur in present suffering. We shy from the suffering we know so well, yet we shy as well from risking change. Present ills, at least, are familiar. To compensate, we may try to puff ourselves up, to drag others down, or to deny anything is wrong. Each of us does it differently, though what we really want may be much the same. We want, quite simply, to be happy. And happiness is not simple.

From a psychoanalytic point of view, when a person can work and love freely, things are going well. Finding meaning and purpose in life helps happiness. Yet meaning and purpose and righteous certitude can be self-soothing delusions, expedient ignorance seized upon by the wish to avoid suffering. Happiness is illusory in the face of a grimmer reality: the common misery of humankind. How can one be happy when sickness and aging are inevitable? When random terrors, calculated cruelties, and lost loves can tear a life apart? When, despite all aspiration and effort, as Macbeth insists, "All our yesterdays have lighted fools the way to dusty death"? Is life, indeed, "a tale told by an idiot, full of sound and fury, signifying nothing"?

While Freud might nod assent, the Buddha has a different answer.

From a Buddhist point of view, happiness ensues the seeing clearly of what is. That grimmer reality of Macbeth and of existentially dismayed psychoanalysis is itself a delusion, one more veil obscuring the clarity of things-as-they-are. To find that clarity requires a change in the notion of what happiness is, and so a change in the notion of who one is and how one is in the world. Such a change at first seems inconceivable, because it transcends all one's past conceptions of the way things are, of what's what and who's who. Such a change requires reconsidering the naïve self who poses the terms of the question.

Asked whether there is a self or no self, it is said, the Buddha responded by silence, with a smile. The terms of the question are ill-founded inasmuch as a declarative answer would perpetuate conceptualization, and ultimately enlightened perception is beyond such concepts as *self* and *no-self*.

A contemporary monk remarks that under meditative concentration "the convention of personality starts to unfold into energetic patterns—patterns that are ephemeral but kammically potent when they're held onto . . . You experience yourself more like an energetic sphere of sensitivity than as a six-foot tall vertebrate who's a man or a woman . . . The mind itself becomes different . . . part of what's going on . . . [not] some separate thing that thinks and decides."*

Dethroned from the seat of rationality is the regal "I," the Cartesian potentate of "I think, therefore I am." My actions (*kamma* in Pali, *karma* in Sanskrit) matter, because they are causes that generate effects. Their effects can make things better, or worse, both for myself and for those around me. Importantly, holding onto "I" in an effort to forestall change and to preserve permanence is a fool's errand—surely lighting the way to dusty death. I indubitably die. Simultaneously, where there is no "I," there is no one to die.

How do I ("I") know ("know")? Presumably, one can know by directly experiencing what's going on, through the sustained practice of attending within. I, writing these words, can lay no claim to such direct knowing. Like you, I must ponder the possibilities. The Buddha cautioned against accepting his teaching on faith, just as no goldsmith should accept a shiny metal as gold until he assays it himself. The challenge is find out for oneself. Look and see. Attend within.

Is the invitation to attend within the same for Buddhism and for psychoanalysis? The counsel of both is to examine the turnings of the mind. The goal of each is to change oneself in order to live with diminished suffering, in happiness. Yet Buddhism's invitation is more radical, in that its meditative method becomes part and parcel of a way of being in the world, a way of knowing and dealing with one's fellows, a way of ethical comportment and refined motivation. In contrast, the more modest invitation of psychoanalysis is to examine together as analyst and analysand the flow of experience, opening in consequence of such examination unforeseen possibilities of forming and unforming how one is.

Accepting either of these different invitations, however, confronts one immediately with dilemmas of desire. Desire to stay the same contends with desire to change.* Desire to stay the same denies the inevitability of perpetual difference; acceptance of (not desire to) change might permit a paradoxical sameness in change. Desire for security—more of the same—wrestles desire for the novel satisfactions of difference.* Desire for a fortress self arouses desire to break free. Part of me desires to live forever. Yet part of me knows better. Nothing lasts forever. Nothing stays the same.

So begins, in part, the old, old message of the Buddha. Part of the first noble truth is that everything changes. Impermanence is our human plight. Each of us must suffer sickness, aging, and death. Nobody gets out alive.

The second noble truth finds the root of suffering in desire—the quality of desire that is clinging, possessive, self-cherishing, nourished by the three "poisons" of greed, hatred, and ignorance. Clinging, the attachment to keeping things the same, leads inevitably to, or inevitably is itself, suffering.

Third: Cessation of clinging allows cessation of suffering. Clinging denies impermanence. Nonattachment permits freedom.

Fourth: There is a way to abandon clinging and so, without suffering, to see things as they are. That way is the eightfold path.

The Buddha's message becomes, then, an experiment to try for oneself. There is in the teaching no zeal to convert, no demand for faith, just an invitation to reflect. Does the inevitability of suffering seem obvious? Is selfish desire the plausible root of suffering? Accordingly, to abandon clinging is to abandon suffering? How to find out for oneself?

The means to find out, the noble eightfold path, addresses one's entire way of being in the world. We share human capacities, and can develop them aright. First, right understanding recognizes causality and choice, in that how you conduct your life can increase or decrease suffering for yourself and others. Second, right mindedness decreases suffering by recognizing illusory doubts and false substitutes for what they are. Third, right speech causes no harm, for words can poison, wound, and kill. Fourth, right bodily conduct hurts no one, neither by sex nor by violence to oneself or others, be it gross or subtle. Fifth, right livelihood benefits the world without exploitation. Sixth, right effort sustains determination to pursue the path—it's work. Seventh, right attentiveness assures relating to the flow of experience mindfully, with meditative awareness. And eighth, right concentration permits singleness of purpose: the liberation of oneself and all sentient beings.

So stands, in part, the old, old message of the Buddha.

For a Buddhist, an aid to right concentration's singleness of purpose might be to join a monastery, the better to focus day in and day out on the extirpation of clinging. The community shares the goal and lives life on the path toward that goal: the cessation of suffering, and concomitantly enlightenment, the seeing of things as they are. A further development is the realization that your suffering is my suffering. One pursues the path not just for one's own enlightenment, but for the enlightenment of all sentient beings. All are related. We are all in this world together.

By comparison to the monastery, secular psychoanalysis must seem a partial and limited endeavor, even if doctor and patient meet an unusually frequent five times a week for more than a few years. How could it be otherwise?

And yet, the two practices share premises, if not the same roof. Both recognize suffering, and both find clinging at play in suffering. For psychoanalysis, the clinging may be a largely unconscious adhesion to old habits of being; the suffering may nominally have less to do with the inevitabilities of sickness, aging, and death than with the frustrations and disappointments of everyday life.

Both practices propose to alter habitual clinging by, as it were, attending pointedly to aspects of experience. Psychoanalysis shares right understanding's notion that actions trace lineaments of cause and effect, and that each of us has a measure of free will by which to choose and act. The right mindedness of psychoanalysis is to assess belief and underlying motivation. The principal mode of psychoanalysis is talking; its right speech is not blaming or judgmental, but an expression of how the talkers care (or fail to care) for one's, and one another's, well-being. A professional assumption of right bodily conduct is that there be no sex, oftentimes no touching: this the better to open the possibility of touching by words. Psychoanalysis itself may lay claim to right livelihood as a "helping" profession; under its purview is how work affects life. Its right effort is to give the therapeutic work its committed chance; its right concentration is to keep in mind its goals. And right attentiveness? What is attending within?

Start psychoanalytically. Stop to notice where you are. There is the outer place, the world out there with its impingements of sound and sight, smell, taste, and physical feeling. There is the boundary place of the body, defining inside and outside, though tenuously, since the inside feelings of the body may be regarded as outside impingements. What regards them? The inner place, the "I," with its memories and associations, its likes and dislikes, its urges and fears. The inner place is "my" mind.

The peculiar, really baffling phenomenon is that I can mind my mind. Even as my experience flows along in its automaticity of one thing perpetually leading to the next, if I pause to regard myself, my experience expands to include a vantage point seemingly outside myself. The experience is not so different from when, as the dreamer of the dream, I watch myself as an actor in the dream. I am myself, and outside myself, all at once. How can it be that an eye see itself?

For an eye to see itself, according to early psychoanalytic theory, there must be a mirror. The metaphorical mirror, of course, was the analyst, who could, with objectivity and neutrality, reflect the limpid truth. But the contemporary analyst is no less a fluctuating bundle of experience than is the patient. When today's certainty can become tomorrow's foolery, is there no vantage point from which to discern what's what?

The analyst and analysand create such a vantage point between them.* It belongs to neither and both. Each has a capacity to reflect inwardly. By psychoanalytic pact, they agree to reflect more intensively on the mind of the analysand. They talk, minding the flow of words with their whorls of images, thoughts, and feelings. What each specifically sees, the other cannot, because each is different, each unique. Nonetheless, what both jointly see, what both (if only temporarily) take as plausible and true, provides that vantage point wherefrom the two are the same. Same and different, different and same. Though you can never be me, you can know my being deeply and well.

We notice, taking "me" as the subject of attention from that psychoanalytic vantage point outside both ourselves, my little lies and excuses, my motivations, hopes, fears, habits of thought, patterns of relatedness. We notice, in effect, my past and present actions and the consequences of those actions. My analyst models and amplifies this strategy of attending within, this taking leave of oneself the better to see oneself. We build up, over time from our vantage point, a complex and variegated view of "me." Simultaneously, both of us must experience and be apart from that "me" in order to see it. And by being apart, by having the reflective distance provided by attending within, "I" gain leverage over "me." I have some room to change, some greater choice as to what to do to feel better. I can better choose, the better to live.

And what is a good life? If we have attended carefully and well, we have noticed that greed and its variants cloak deprivation (wanting begets further wanting); hate makes hate; denial's saying no won't make it so. When those around me are happier, so am I. What we want, at base, is the same. How we find it is, for each of us, different, yet the same.

The attending within of psychoanalysis focuses on the interconnected thoughts and feelings that give rise to one's sense of self. Analyst and patient intensively review *in vivo* how beliefs and feelings come to be, how actions generate consequences, what getting better means in the context of an individual life and in an individual relationship. Their review requires a letting go of self to provide a vantage point from which to regard self.

Who is it who watches from that vantage point? It cannot be a little me within, a unifying homunculus in charge of the sensory control panels, because then that homunculus requires its own inner watching homunculus, which requires its own again, on and ever in infinite regression.* Who is watching is undefined, always out of sight seemingly just ahead around the next bend, always eluding objectification. Who is watching is, in a very real sense, no one at all.

Perpetually I cognize the world and my place at the center of my world. To the extent that I can stop, I succeed at not recognizing (re-cognizing) myself. I am free, but I am no longer I, or merely I. Psychoanalytic attention utilizes this slippage, this introspective double-take, to provide room for change.

So, too, does the right attention of the Buddha. While analytic attention is implicit in its practice and contributes to an amplified understanding of who and how one is, Buddhism's explicit practice of meditation amplifies the attentive faculty itself. That faculty has two modal aspects, concentration and contemplation. Concentrative techniques invite the mind to focus one-pointedly, say, on the breath, and to notice the arising and passing away of thoughts and feelings while returning again and again to the object of concentration. Contemplative techniques, in a sense, concentrate on negotiating the experiential flow itself, its arising and passing away, its invitations toward craving or aversion or denial, its cascading portrayals of reality. And the practice of these techniques is something like practicing the piano, requiring diligence and persistence to improve skill.

Right attentiveness, the mindfulness developed through meditation, is not an end in itself, but a means toward understanding how things are, and everythings' interrelatedness. Attentiveness reveals the subtle ways clinging manifests itself, coloring the world, obscuring clarity. What attentiveness reveals can be let go. Cessation of clinging includes, in a subtle yet profound way, letting go of one's self.

Whereas the psychoanalytic pair focuses on personality the better to loosen its strictures, the meditative adept may more leapfrog over personality the better to ascertain its place in reality.

Imagine a play on a theatrical stage. By virtue of the necessary "suspension of disbelief"* you forget the darkened theatre and how you got there. You watch the play immersed in the action, the characters, the setting, the plot. You identify with the hero. Your busybody analyst (conveniently seated at your elbow) unsettles your immersion by interjecting comments and reactions. You decide to confine those to regularly scheduled intermissions, when you discuss twists of plot and motivation and possible alternative scenarios. Together, you watch what you do and do not attend to. Your reflections, you discover, affect what happens on stage. And then, perhaps, with luck and more concentrated attention, you begin to see that the play and you and your analyst are characters immersed in a larger play that includes the first. The larger play, too, is an artifact of attention. The larger play, too, takes place in an unattended darkness. You can leave your seat, step back into the darkness, go where there is no one to watch, because in the darkness, you are no one.

THE CONSULTING ROOM*

The room is on a high floor of a masonry building, high enough up that despite the newer skyscrapers nearby the room's three windows reflect the vaulting arch of changing sky. The windows look south over the island city like the bridge of a ship over its prow. The river to the right and the river to the left meet in the south, the city afloat between their streams steaming along with the hum of traffic and people and the clouds scudding overhead through time.

Inside the empty room is silence. The windows hush most outside sound. Windowpanes let sunlight fall in shifting rectangles on the patterned rug: blue and orange filigrees brighten over their pool of Persian red. Opposite the windows is a wall of books, floor to high ceiling, wall to wall except for just at the center where the bookshelves frame a door, polished dark wood, brass knob unpolished except where hands have touched it.

Opposite the door beneath the windows rest two reclining armchairs with a lamp table between them. On the table, frozen in mid-gallop, is a Chinese bronze horse. The woodgrain of the table makes undulating streams between the chairs.

To the left chair's right is a low round table where a red diode on the telephone's answering machine blinks persistently, once each second. Along the wall toward the books is a leather couch. A cushion forms a headrest facing the books. On the cushion is an opened paper cocktail napkin, a curious antimacassar.

To the right chair's left, along the wall facing the couch, a low bookshelf serves as a stand for a large opened dictionary and a small clock. A desk holds books and mail and manila folders. From the desk lamp hangs a spherical crystal fob—of the sort found on a chandelier—that contains in upside-down orbitally-curved reflection the entire room. On the wall are two framed diplomas and a black-and-white photograph of the sea crashing against coastal rocks beneath a looming sky. In the room the crashing sea makes no sound. From across the empty room the red diode, steady as a lighthouse, blinks soundlessly.

The doorknob turns. The door opens.

In comes an older man in a suit. He checks his appointment book, listens to his messages. He glances at the clock, rises to cross the room and opens the one door, then another soundproofed door just beyond it. He beckons from the doorway into the waiting room beyond and returns to his chair.

A younger man, wearing shorts and a bicycle helmet, comes in, closing the doors behind him. He sits on the couch, takes off his shoes, and places his helmet on the floor beside them. He lies back on the couch with his hands clasped over his eyes.

A minute passes, then another.

He twists on the couch, and groans, audibly.

The older man asks, "So. Where are you?"*

"Dunno. Guess I'm bummed out."

"By anything in particular?"

"Not really. Just back to baseline, I suppose. I did a few laps around the park, and now I'm here."

"What was it like, doing the laps?"

"You know, maybe that's why I'm bummed out. Usually I can just get into the rhythm of it, sort of pump along, keep my momentum going despite the hills and all. Like when I get to the crest of that panther hill—where that panther statue looks like it's about to leap down onto you from its little cliff?"

"Um-hmm."

"It's always a kick to get to the top and then zoom away from the panther."

"A successful escape! You get absorbed in it. It grabs your attention."

"Only not today. Today I don't even glance at the panther. Today it's 'What am I goddam doing riding around in circles in the park?' I mean, there I am, pumping away, with these other bikers trying to pass me like we're in a race, and all the joggers drenched in sweat looking like it's the first pang of acute appendicitis, and I'm wondering 'What the fuck am I doing here?'"

"What's your answer? What were you doing there?"

"What am I doing here? It's like talking about this stuff is just more going around in circles. I don't know what I'm doing."

"You're angry."

"Sure, I'm angry. How long have I been coming here? Three times a week for two years? And in some ways I'm right back at Square One, where I was when Karen left me. Nothing seems like it's worth doing, I am a particular piece of worthless shit, and nobody cares anyway . . . It's not just anger. I feel frustrated and overwhelmed. It reminds me of that time in junior high when they pushed me to do the school play as well as the damned newsletter and chess club and everything else, and I just crumpled and fell down and cried on the floor. God, how embarrassing. That was one of the worst, so humiliating. But I wish I could cry like that now."

"Can you?"

"No. I can't."

"Why not?"

"Well for one thing, I'm twenty-eight, not fourteen or whatever. And it'd still be embarrassing, to cry in front of you—even though I have. Besides, what good would it do?"

"I don't get it. If it wouldn't do any good, why do you wish you could cry like that now?"

"I don't want to wallow in self-pity."

"You're afraid that's what your crying would look like to me?"

"Maybe it's more that it would look like wallowing to me."

"But it's not just wallowing. You wish you could cry like that now. There's some feeling you're after?"

"Huh. I guess so. Let's see . . . You know what? I think when I was fourteen I also felt free. I mean, after my little fall-down performance—should've been an audition—I knew that there was no way I was going to have to be in that play. I showed them I had my own limits, so I was free of the play, and free to choose what I wanted to do. At least I was freer than when I just tried to accommodate everybody. Even though I'd embarrassed myself, and the other kids thought I was a loser, so what, I could go my own way."

"And today? How does the memory work for today?"

"Well, that's the problem, isn't it? It doesn't work for today. I could boo-hoo up a storm here or at home and it doesn't change anything."

"You mean it wouldn't free you to go your own way?"

"I don't see how. Especially since, at this point, I don't know what going my own way is."

"Feeling lousy is not going your own way."

"Okay, so I know what going my own way isn't."

"I'm wondering if the crying might be absorbing, like a way to free your attention from its bummed-out base-line in order to feel better. Like enjoying your escape from the panther when the bike-riding works."

"Only I'm loop-de-looping around the park in the first place in order to distract myself from how lousy I'm feeling. It's a distraction, not some way to fix things. I'm still going around in circles in my life because I don't know where else to go."

"I see. The things that make you feel a little better distract you from finding even better ways to take care of yourself?"

"They distract me from how generally lousy I'm feeling and how I don't know any better how to take care of myself."

"You're stuck going around in circles?"

"That's what it feels like."

"And here, too?"

"Well, sometimes. But I keep coming, don't I? I guess there's hope here. I mean, it does feel like it helps at least to say what's happening. Maybe it just helps me realize what I'm feeling."

"You said you feel like you're back at Square One."

"Well, not entirely. Obviously I'm not suicidal the way I was. And I'm working. I'm plunking—I almost said pumping—away a year and a half now at my job. The sage lawyers of Smith, Caruthers, and So On provide their evening-shift word-processors an endless flow of fascinating legal documents, have I ever mentioned?"

"You're angry."

"I'm at a dead end."

"Are you angry at me?"

"Huh . . . That's interesting. You know, I was going to say no—that I'm not angry at you—but I realize saying I'm not angry would be like angrily shoving you away. Part of me is angry at you. The part of me that wants you to pick me up off the floor and to make everything right and to promise me a worthwhile life."

"The same way you wanted Karen to provide you with all of that."

"Yep, same deal. Of course, it drove her away, and you don't seem to go away. I can't really blame her, though part of me still does. Same part that's angry with you, because you won't—or can't—fix me. In the end, you always leave it up to me. I have to find my own way? Geez . . . You know, as I talk about this stuff now I don't feel angry with you. It's hard to say it, but I feel really fond of you. Like you've been with me, through such a lot."

"And here we are."

"Here we are. Yes. You know, I actually feel better."

"How'd we get here?"

*"Dunno. Must've found some way."**

2.

FINDING EMPTINESS

Holy Avalokiteshvara, the bodhisattva, the great being, spoke to the venerable
Shariputra and said, "Form is emptiness, emptiness is form; emptiness
is not other than form, form too is not other than emptiness." *
—THE HEART SUTRA

FOR YEARS, as part of an effort at daily meditation, I have been practicing a Tibetan visualization* that begins, "In the space before me
appears a white lotus . . ." I am not very good at it. I cannot create in
my mind's eye the three-dimensional cinematic versimilitude I suppose to be the goal. For years, in fact, while I focused on articulating
the form of the white lotus and its cascade of subsequent images,
while I tried to let go the perpetual distractions of peripheral thoughts
and the noisy press of the physical world around, of, and in me, I failed
to notice where the visualization began: in the *space* before me.

How visualize space? Is space visualized a form? Is space emptiness?

I try logic. Space is the absence that is present that is nothing in
itself. That's confusing. Space cannot be present because being pres-
ent makes it a thing. Space cannot be absent because no thing is absent.
Nothing is absent. Nothing being absent sounds full. Full of nothing?
I'm more confused. The nearest I can figure is that you can't figure.
No figuring must be space? Go figure.

Perhaps, most of the time we are awake, that's just what we are
doing: figuring—and not just in the sense of puzzling out what led to
what and what's going to happen next, but also in the sense of
configuring the world, of forming in mind a whole intricate visualization of what's real and what's not, of who I am and who you are, of
what has happened we can call the past, of what we can expect to call

the future. Memory forms possibility. We are figuring. Even when we dream, we are figuring up a version of awakeness, figuring out what to pay attention to.

Most of the time the figuring works so well we don't even notice we are doing it. That's all right when things go well, but things never go well forever. We find ourselves as if trapped in a movie written and directed by someone else, with some nasty turns of plot. The lure of psychoanalysis is its suggestion that we can begin more to notice how we are doing the figuring, and so begin more and better to direct our own lives. Figure freely, take responsibility for shaping your life. You can change. That's the psychoanalytic view.

The Buddha's view goes further, past the horizon of figuring to where there is no where, no figure. It's not at all that Buddhism avoids taking responsibility for shaping one's life. Indeed, the crucial under-standing of karma (which literally in Sanskrit means "action") is that one's actions in body, speech, and mind have consequences, positive and negative. Understand how you create your own consequences, and you can decrease the negative, increase the positive. Understand clearly, directly from experience. As with psychoanalysis, that's the figuring.

The stupendous, ungrounding further insight of Buddhism is that the curlicues of figuring, the filigrees of thought, lace a void of no figure. Imbuing my thoughts and feelings, generating my precious self to which I cling like life, is emptiness.

> Yet, I shy from emptiness because
> . . . it is so much easier
> to think of our lives,
> as we move under the brief luster of leaves,
> loving what we have,
> than to think of how it is
> such small beings as we
> travel in the dark
> with no visible way
> or end in sight.*

Buddhism lights a way. The dark, the way, and the end entail finding emptiness in form, form in emptiness.

This is a vast realization, this realization of vastness. An inconceivably complex interaction of past actions gives rise to each of us, bobbing along awhile for a lifetime, each of us like a bubble in its seemingly separate orb of awareness, each an orbitally curved reflection of an entire world, all the bubbles together like tumbling froth at the breaking crest of a wave in a far off sea, and that wide sea itself cupped in the spaciousness of a vaulting sky whose darkling depth is without limit. We are buoyed on emptiness.

And what is emptiness? One Buddhist commentator, who translates the Sanskrit *sunyata* as "Voidness," tries to elucidate:

> At this point a few words on "Voidness" may be helpful. When we say "That house is empty," we mean that it contains no occupants; but Buddhist "Voidness" *does not mean absence*. When we say, "That whole block is now empty," we mean there were houses in the block before, but none exist now; but Buddhist "Voidness" *does not mean extinction*. Voidness is difficult to define and describe. We can say a great deal about what Voidness is *not*, but very little about what it *is*. Voidness denotes the relative, flowing, undefinable, and ungraspable nature of all things. Philosophically it represents the illusory and dream-like nature of phenomena; psychologically it signifies a total liberation from all bondage.*

Emptiness is not absence, not extinction. Emptiness is—the Heart Sutra reminds us—form itself. How to find form's emptiness?

I pause. I ask again what is the space before me. Like the air around me, I cannot see it. Unlike the air around me, nothing is there to see. I can feel the air against my skin; not so space. I can hear the air, from its harsh wind's whistle to its soft Brownian whish against my eardrums; not so with silent space. Air carries me smells and tastes; never does space.

Physical space comprises absence, which is not emptiness. It *is* somewhere in relation to what else is there. Here and there.

Temporal space comprises extinction, which is not emptiness. It demarcates what is from what was and what will be. Now and then.

Philosophy's shimmering abstractions are grounded in psychological space; they are forms in my mind. They require *me* to form them, to make relations between thoughts within—and without: to make relations between you and me and our hard-edged world. I map a psychological space with "me" at the center of my orb of awareness. You and me. This "me" is a form in psychological space. If this form, indeed, is empty, behind the face that looks at me is there no one? Does being free of me free me to a total liberation from all bondage?

Let us consider these forms in a search for emptiness in form, form in emptiness. Physical space is not emptiness, yet emptiness is there: empty of here and there. The space of time is not emptiness, yet time is empty: empty of now and then. Psychological space is not emptiness, yet emptiness appears: empty of you and me. Let us trace these forms, like the nightime tracks of shooting stars over that wave-tossed sea, across that vaulting sky. These forms themselves somehow are manifest emptiness.

Empty of here and there. The physicists* tell us space is everywhere, weirdly cloaked by the seeming solidity of things. Look hard, and the obdurate rock becomes a lattice of molecules—a great many of them, to be sure, but tiny constellated specks locked in a pattern of repulsion and attraction holding between them nothing, that is, space. Look harder, at a single atom of one of these miniscule molecules. Its nucleus is like a fly in the cathedral of its hovering field of probabilistic electrons. And within the nucleus, between its interlocked protons and neutrons, is space.

Look harder still, to the subatomic, to quantum strangeness, where particles become waves that act like particles and singular things can be in two places at once and can spontaneously pop into

and out of existence, where the distinction between thing and nothing becomes an indistinct probabilistic guess, where quantum foam
(like the foam at the crest of a breaking wave) creates a temporary
place in, once again, space. A particle may be a brief manifestation of
a string gyrating in eleven dimensions of space and time. Out of such
nothingness comes something, and something to nothing returns.
Subatomic particles appear and disappear, into and out of the physical space between them. The physical space is itself no particle, but
what lies between particles: the absence of particles.

Emptiness is not absence. Emptiness is not bounded, even by
eleven dimensions. Emptiness is not between this and that, if this and
that themselves are also fundamentally empty.

Perhaps we have been looking through the wrong end of a telescope. Reverse it; examine the heavens. Immediately we see how far
far can be. Ninety-three million miles to the sun is too far to walk!
The sun dwarfs our sister planets, some bigger, some littler, yet all,
like our earth, distant specks orbiting in a space almost cozy compared to the cold remoteness of the stars. And the stars cluster into
galaxies, the distances between the stars as nothing compared to the
distances between the galaxies. Space, and more space, empty of
matter.

Yet space is not empty. Spanning space is energy, matter's Ein-
steinian transform, in the form of waves radiating in various ampli-
tudes and frequencies from multitudinous sources to multifarious
destinations. Light, heat, X-rays, gravity—forces here affect the far-
off there, and the there comes here. Space is not empty. Space suspends all matter and energy; it cloaks vastly more dark matter and
dark energy—dark, because we cannot see or account for it by what
we now know. We study the cosmology of space the better to know,
and always find limits of knowing. What we cannot know in any usual
sense lies, perhaps, across the span of space, beyond the edge of
space—in emptiness?

Crossing space takes time.

Empty of now and then. The fixed speed of light defines space: space is the distance light travels in a given time. Space is a measure of time, time of space. Meridians of longitude mark off distances on the surface of the earth not in miles but in hours and minutes and seconds. Space and time intertwine: physics finds neither space, nor time, but space-time.*

Hours and minutes and seconds are not constant. Accelerate my body toward the speed of light and my moment becomes your century. Our clocks fail to synchronize. Time and space fold and bend. The curved three-dimensional orbit of our earth around our sun reveals itself to be a straight line in four-dimensional space-time.

Let the sun explode; for us the calamitous event does not happen until there elapses the eight minutes travel time required for the light of the explosion to reach us. If no light, then no explosion. Until the flash of light, the event is for us in an elsewhere that does not yet exist. If the flash occurs for us at all, it has already popped into our absolute future absolutely leading, cause and effect, to the having-happened fixity of our absolute past. We surmise the eight minutes to account for our coherently absolute reality, oblivious of an inconceivable elsewhere. We exist as if at the neck of an hourglass, future streaming to past; because we cannot go faster than light, we are trapped forever inside the glass. Outside the glass is elsewhere, outside all possible futures.

The past, like the ripples from a pebble dropped in a pond, recedes farther and farther from us. We train our telescope the farthest we can see. We see stars whose light traverses space and more space for thousands and millions of years to flicker in our momentary now revealing what occurred so far away so very long ago. The light from the farthest reaches of space reveals how things were at the beginning of time.

We peer out to the very edge of the universe, to the farthest ripple emanating from what we surmise to be the big bang that started it all. This primal explosion was a singularity, that is, an ultimately originary point-event. It did not occur in space; from it erupted all of space and all of energy and matter. It took place here and everywhere else all at once, because all the separate locations of the universe were then overwhelmingly condensed into the same location.* Likewise, it did not occur at a given point in time; with it, time began. The singularity held all points as one point, all moments as one moment. There can be, the theory holds, no time before time, no space outside of space. Before and outside are indefinable, an impenetrable elsewhere.

We are forced to stop, unable to see beyond the time and space that comprise our universe and us in it. Before the beginning nothing was begun. Nothing is outside the universe that itself stipulates inside and outside, here and there, then and when. Outside, where there is no outside, no inside, no there but elsewhere, neither distance nor presence nor absence, neither before nor after, no birth, no extinction, we find, perhaps, unmediated emptiness.

Yet emptiness, as understood in the Heart Sutra, is not long ago and far away outside and before some originary big bang. Emptiness is not elsewhere, but here and now in the little bang of fleeting form each passing moment. Though empty of time, emptiness is timed by the swell of breath, the heartbeat, the red diode flashing second by second. The venerable Avalokiteshvara found, "Form is emptiness, emptiness is form; emptiness is not other than form, form too is not other than emptiness. Likewise, feelings, perceptions, mental formations, and consciousness are all empty . . . all phenomena are emptiness; they are without defining characteristics; they are not born, they do not cease; they are not defiled, they are not undefiled; they are not deficient, they are not complete . . . There is no eye, no ear, no nose, no tongue, no body, and no mind. There is no form, no sound, no smell, no taste, no texture, and no mental objects . . . There is no ignorance, there is no extinction of ignorance . . . no aging and death and no extinction of aging and death. Likewise, there is no suffering, origin, cessation, or path; there is no wisdom, no attainment, and even no nonattainment."* Avalokiteshvara found emptiness in form, even in the form of concepts, beyond beyondness. Time's form, too, is empty.

Rightly understood, emptiness gives rise to form; form manifests emptiness.* Forms do exist, but without any *intrinsic* essence. I do, indeed, find myself embodied and minded, bruisable in a solid world where one thing always leads to the next. Time alters form. What was gives rise to what is, which falls into place as what will have been from some point past. Gasses condense into planets. Planetary seas cool into organic broth where molecules complexly interact forming, unforming down through vast time. A spermatozoan finds an ovum. And here I am, impermanent, temporary, for the time being a confluence of past concatenations soon to subside into other forms. For the time being, formed, I am.

Empty of you and me. Let the cosmos take care of itself. I put down the telescope to ask who has been doing the looking.

When I remember to pay attention, when I try to notice myself by attending within, what do I find? Am I emptiness? Anything but, it would at first seem. My eyelid itches, my stomach growls, back aches; nose smells soup (Maryland crab chowder), mouth waters; thoughts harangue to stay at the keyboard; the fan of the space heater whirrs in my ears; eyes wander over snow-covered ivy outside my window stopped by the hollowed-eye gaze of the green-man garden sculpture who never blinks and I pull my gaze away lest he start to seem accusatory. I find myself in the midst of the season, the day, the moment, the recollection of how I got here, the expectation of what's to come.

But do I find myself in the midst of all this, or is being amidst what I am? Shut down my experience and I disappear into dreamless sleep or death; opening experience opens me as a this in relation to that, as the crossing over from present into past of all my thoughts and sensations, as a being that can witness itself only in relation to particular situations. What's out there becomes what's in me, my world, me of it and it of me. You might not think the stony eye accusatory, or care for crab soup. That's your world. I ate the soup. Crab soup writes these words.

One thing leads to the next and the phone rings and I pick up a bit of conversation and leave it to connect with what will come later, good-bye. I busily place words and thoughts and things where I think they should go and process and modulate and digest and tidy up. I am a squirrel storing nuts, a dog barking to guard the door, an uneasy miscreant before the stony gaze; or hardening my heart, I am the green man himself like a stone. I am the chill of the snow, its cold crept under the door, sliding beneath the hot breath of the heater.

Take away my guises, and I am no one. I am not separate from experience. I find myself only in relationship,* only in alterity, altering as the world alters, without separate fixity, with no intrinsic constancy. It is not that I go from one guise to the next, like a versatile actor, a master of make-up and disguise. The idea of the masterful player, constant through guises, is itself another guise, another passing thought I (sooner or later) entertain in relation to my wishes and fears in their experiential flux. Part of me does want to petrify like a rock, to be perpetual and unvanquished, declaiming "In the fell clutch of circumstance/ I have not winced nor cried aloud./ Under the bludgeonings of chance/ My head is bloody but unbowed."* I remember the poem from schooldays, an orienting piece of memory; I remember how to feel my way into the valiant part. But the part is wearing, performance after grim-jawed performance. So many other parts beckon, with their songs and laughter and tears. I am all over the place, everywhere and nowhere.

I can find myself only in guise, only in dualistic relation to particular times and places and persons: me here, you and the rest there. I am not in disguise, because behind disguise hides by implication the undisguised. Whenever I am, whatever I am, if I am, I am in guise. Behind my guises, in the psychological space of my undulating mind, do I there find emptiness?

One guise that attempts to look behind itself is that of analysand. Another is that of meditator. Both analysand and meditator commit to practices of attention.

Meditation, in all its variations, is usually taught as a practice. The practice may be focused and concentrative, or contemplatively present and mindful. It may be inquisitively reflective or creatively transformative or lovingly heart-centered.* Whatever the emphasis, meditation requires setting time aside to practice repeated and disciplined attention to attention. One reminds oneself to practice daily. One re-minds oneself through daily practice.

Psychoanalysis, though practiced, is not usually thought of as a practice. Yet undergoing psychoanalysis requires setting time aside, regularly and repeatedly, to notice the nature of one's own attention. It takes time to re-mind oneself, with the analyst as a reminder, session after session, whether you feel like going that day or not, time after time until it becomes just part of what you're doing, always some small part of yourself thinking about what you're doing, thinking about what you're going to tell your analyst, noticing what you're experiencing at some slight remove so that you're observing yourself while being yourself all at the same time, time after time. Being in analysis develops the practice of reflexive awareness. Often awareness recounts more of the same; sometimes awareness opens to what's new.

Meditative attention serves to still the mind, to clarify how chattering words and proliferating thoughts can obscure what's as new as it is old: limpid and bare awareness, simple being.

Psychoanalytic attention reveals that we do listen to some words assiduously, while others we do our best to ignore. At first, session after session, each analysand recites, in effect, a published script, "*Who I Am,* by Me,"—no major revisions allowed, however monotonous the story may be. We each enact our handful of roles, our cherished self-states, and cast the analyst appropriately. We labor our lives away to maintain the form of who-I-am in all its stolidity, good points and bad. Stolidly, we act much the same day by day, generating and confronting the same old problems, relieved by tinctures of the same pleasures. Listening to the wrong words can feel dangerous, like a shout of "Fire!" in a crowded theatre. The analyst's words we fear, yet hope to hear, are, in effect, "*You are not simply who you think you are.*" ("*Fire!*") "*You can let your self go.*" ("*Fire!*") "*You are free to revise the text.*" ("*Fire!*") These words are "Fire!" because they threaten the conflagration of the familiar self. They raise the spectre of not being me, of my extinction by death. I dread that not-being as if it meant being torn to pieces by a pack of wolves. Yet being incinerated, being extinct, being torn apart, are imaginable self-states. Each entails being something in some way (including the way of being someone dead and gone). Not-being-any-me, in uncanny contrast, negates self-states. The shift is from transitive to intransitive: from not being something, simply to being; from describable, to indescribable. Such simple being is psychoanalytically accessible to the extent that analysand and analyst can forgo variable self-states of "me."

The meditator, by a different and perhaps more direct route, ponders the puzzling words that emptiness is form and form emptiness, that there is neither death nor the extinction of death, so as to come to a first-hand experience of the being that is not-being: no ponderer, just pondering; neither pondering, nor not; no first, no hand; no face to face. Then the meditator quite embodied rises from the cushion and goes about business of and in the world. Yet the nature of the world and of oneself in the world becomes different. One traveler in the high Himalaya puts it well:

> The secret of the mountains is that the mountains simply
> exist, as I do myself: the mountains exist simply, which I
> do not. The mountains have no "meaning," they *are* mean-
> ing; the mountains *are*. The sun is round. I ring with life,
> and the mountains ring, and when I can hear it, there is a
> ringing that we share. I understand all this, not in my mind
> but in my heart, knowing how meaningless it is to capture
> what cannot be expressed, knowing that mere words will
> remain when I read it all again, another day.[*]

The meditator and the analysand strive to alter ways of being, and in doing so, mysteriously, each encounters being: the simple, intransitive being of emptiness. The encounter may be more direct for the meditator, but is no less relevant for the analysand.

One well-known psychoanalyst, in fact, writes about mental health as the capacity to "stand in the spaces" between self-states, that is, the capacity to feel like one continuous self while experiencing the multiplicity of the ways one can be. The continuity of self is an illusion (albeit a valuable illusion) obscuring the often contradictory and frequently distasteful ways one habitually finds oneself being in the world. "'Standing in the spaces' is a shorthand way of describing a person's relative capacity to make room at any given moment for subjective reality that is not readily containable by the self he experiences as 'me' at that moment."* I lose myself in the spaces; I am ready to find myself anew.

Someone who could not do this at all might seem brittle or fragile, boring or domineering. Or that someone might be a multiple personality disorder, whose self-states appear unacquainted. Normally, self-states link into an overarching self experienced as coherent and unified. Yet that self, too, for all its self-generated consistency, is a self-state, linked here and there, unlinked elsewhere, tendrils dangling in space. Attending to how this is so requires a kind of mental step backwards, a step back away from self to stand in space. And as the one who stands coalesces into a stander, into another self, whilst the pieces of memory rearrange themselves one steps backwards again into the groundless space one has no eyes to see, no I to know, where there is no footfall, no foot, but emptiness.

If, as analysand and analyst, we leave in abeyance some assiduous treatment plan with its goals and objectives, if we simply meet, the two of us, where are we then? Does it matter what words break the silence of the empty consulting room? Does it matter, as writer and reader, what words lift off the page into meaning? Because you are there, I am not alone. We describe our experience. We pick and choose and inquire what we can know of the experience of the other. We tell each other, we show each other, who we are, only finding who in the telling, even as the telling falls into silence. We pause in emptiness. Meanwhile, inevitably and spontaneously, another self springs up, a bubble out of nowhere, and here I am, pleased to meet you, joined as we are in our world by the walls of a room, or by this page opaque between us. I scratch my head. You scrunch your nose. What do we do now?

How about you read, and I'll meditate.

When I set out to visualize "In the space before me appears a white lotus . . ." I remind myself not to rush to the lotus, first to attend to the emptiness of space, and next to attend to the peculiarities of "before me." Letting go for the moment the question of who is doing this visualizing, when I visualize "before me," that "me" is a visualization. Visualizing thusly generates an endless concatenation of duality: viewer and viewed, subject and object, inner and outer, here and there, now and then. What I have is my usually unconsidered assumption of the the real world around me with me in the middle of it. No one is visualizing, I justifiably assume, because this is real. "I" cannot be a visualization when no one is visualizing—unless, while no one notices (least of all myself) I am a self-perpetuating visualization of myself. "I" am a tag-along in the wake of the onrushing experience that whorls "me" in its wake. It just seems to happen that I keep showing up. I am, indeed, real, but hard reality is no longer quite what I took it for. Looking harder, I find emptiness.

Beyond duality, I am neither real nor not, neither I nor not-I. In duality, I can catch myself like a rapid-fire sequence of photographs, each true to how I was at the moment the photograph was taken, none of them true to what was beyond the surface of the moment. Who I am becomes yesterday's photograph of who I was. Going beyond the sequential moment means going beyond duality's now and then, beyond presence and absence. When I look in the mirror, my face becomes "obverse without a reverse."* My form is empty. My self, like everything else, is merely an arising and passing away, an exfoliating spacious emptiness providing room to grow.

Yet you are here to listen, changing with me. We have the immense good fortune to encounter one another, to behold each other in the moment not just as solitary selves, but as companions, as fellows-well-met. We glimpse in each other the Buddha within. The moment perpetually dissolves away, as does everything the moment seems to hold: you and me and the world around us. The clear-eyed child you were is gone, and the you I gaze on is in rapid pursuit. And the I who gazes goes, too, is gone even now, to, in, of emptiness.

My experience is a jumble of passing pieces, the memories, dreams, reflections* I reform continually into my own memories, dreams, perceptions. I am forming unforming reforming. Death is already here in the passing of each moment, while each moment, miraculously, I am born anew. My freeing choice is in how to piece myself together, even while the pieces change. My perpetual choice is in whom I might make of myself now, with you, given this moment's associative span of experience, given all that we can turn our attention to. We are our consciousness. The turnings of attention are, or can moreso be, our choice. We dwell in spaciousness, with room to choose how to live, how to open being. We are emptiness.

OPENING

"So it's the same old story. I finish my shift at midnight, pretty tired and wiped out. I bike home, have popcorn and a beer, hit the sack by 1:00 and am out like a light. Next thing I know I'm awake, looking at four one four, 4:14, on the damned digital clock."

"How were you feeling?"

"I was feeling like not being awake, of course. Still just drawn-out tired and furious that the clickety-clack thoughts were started. I knew right off it was a lost cause. Part of it was the heat. I was drenched in sweat with the one clammy sheet glued to me, so I peeled it off and sat there cursing the landlord. I don't think I told you, but I think he's trying to sell the building for one of those loft conversions so he fixed up the front and in the process painted all my windows shut. So the only air he leaves me is the teeny vent at the top of my dirty skylight. I wake up thinking I'm going to have to go out on the fire escape and razor-blade the windows open myself since he'll never do it and meanwhile what if there were a fire in the place? I'm supposed to try crashing through these windows with the chickenwire set into the glass? I'm already basting up there like a rotisserie special because all the heat in the building rises to the top floor and little did I think when he repaired the roof from leaking all over me that he'd insulate it so I'm wearing a fiberglass parka in the middle of summer."

"It's like you're telling me the 'clickety-clack' thoughts now as you speak."

"*Maybe. I suppose so. It's like the one thought just leads to the next and before I know it I'm off and running—but going nowhere.*"

"*Your insomnia is sticky, too, then. It's like a chain of thoughts dragging you along?*"

"*Except this time I did something about it. I got up, pulled some clothes on out of the pile beside my bed, grabbed my helmet and started down the five flights of stairs except, wouldn't you know, the light was out on the fifth floor landing so I'm threading my way in the dark through all these boxes and paint cans and junk that Francesco has left outside his door. Christ! Can you imagine a fireman trying to get up there with all that equipment they have to wear and everything? We'd all get roasted because he'd get his oxygen tank stuck on Francesco's shark—he's got this shark mobile made out of chain-link fence, see, that's hanging in the stairwell? Roasted for the sake of art. I should talk to Francesco. Hell, I should talk to the landlord. Who's going to buy the building no matter how nice it looks on the outside when they can't even get up the stairs without being bitten by a shark? Not that I want anyone to buy the building. If someone buys the building they'll probably gut it and stick in an elevator and make all the lofts fancy floor-throughs and Francesco and I and the shark and everyone else will be camped out front on the truck loading dock with all our stuff and nowhere to go.*"

"*It's interesting you remembered to take your helmet.*"

"*My helmet? My bicycle helmet? That's almost automatic. Why is that interesting?*"

"*It strikes me that a lot of what you're talking about is protection—being protected from fire, from danger, injury. Or being protected from having nowhere to live.*"

"*You're trying to tell me you don't run around worrying about these things? Joking aside—I know you don't worry, or I think you don't worry, at least in the way I'm talking about it*[*]—*but you know it's not like I'm always worrying, either.*"

"*What makes you think I don't worry?*"

"*Huh? Well, if you do, I mean like me, don't we have the blind leading the blind here?*"

"*I'm supposed to be leading you?*"

"*Well, not exactly, I guess. I suppose I do look up to you, though.*"

"And I let you?"

"It's not so bad. Maybe I need someone I can look up to."

"Pleased to oblige—for the time being."

"I thank you for keeping your worries to yourself. Besides, it's not like I'm consumed by worry. Like I do know there are smoke alarms in the building even if it isn't sprinklered, and if I really had to I could bash through those chicken-wire windows in order to get to the fire escape. That's so cheap, to stick in wire I suppose so that if the window cracks it'll hold together and they won't have to repair it for a hundred years. And we know if push came to shove Dad would always bail me out financially, not that I'd want to have to ask him to. It's bad enough he pays over half your fee."

"How do you mean?"

"I wish I could just pay it myself, but since you make eight times more an hour than I do and I can't work twenty-four hours a day and still sleep and bring in those dreams you're so interested in, I'm in a bind."

"How does it make you feel about yourself?"

"Like the apron strings—guess the phrase doesn't work so well for a father—like the apron strings aren't cut, so I'm dependent and I wish I weren't."

"How would it feel to be independent? Like you wouldn't need a helmet?"

"Aha! The psychoanalytic connection! Let's see. You do have something. Obviously, I don't want to get sideswiped by some taxi and smear my brains all over some sidewalk. But more generally, it is like I'm afraid I can't manage on my own. I need protection from everything I can't control. It's the same old fix, isn't it? When do I get to start feeling like a grown-up? Will you raise me up, O Surrogate Daddy?"

"And the same old fix: wishing that someone can do it for you."*

"My mother dying was not a lot of help."

"You didn't get enough of those apron strings."

"But that was, let's see, fourteen years ago. How about now? I was telling you how I did do something rather than just lie there in the sweaty sheets, swelter-ing in my hot-box fix."

"Yes?"

"So obviously it's bicycling, since I brought my helmet. I did manage to get down the stairs without breaking my neck, and untangle the bike from the other

ones at the foot of the stairs. Remember when I was the only one who had a bike? There's that little space behind the double front door where the slot is hacked through for the mail basket? That was just fine until four other people decided to get bikes, too, and now they all have to be sort of piled up on top of one another so you can get past the front door at all. Christ, it wouldn't be the shark, the fireman would take half a step through the front door and be buried in bicycles!"

"I'm exhausted just hearing about it. Were you so tired out by getting down the stairs that you went back up and fell asleep?"

"Very funny. But I'm just about to get to the change. This is important."

"The change? Okay."

"So to get the bike out the front door you have to sort of stand it on its rear wheel holding it by the handlebars with one hand, and with the other hand reach around and open the half door—which is spring-loaded to shut, just to keep things interesting—and wheel the bike out turning it slightly in order to get the handlebars through. While I'm doing this I'm once again drenched in sweat and ready to roar like a lion if anything else gets in my way, but it doesn't, and I get through the door onto the loading dock, and the door slams shut behind me. Then it hits me: this puff of wind."

"A puff of wind?"

"I mean, what I'm trying to get across is the change. I burst out of my jam-packed building like a maniac waving a bicycle as a murder weapon, and puff, this gentle wind strokes my face and body. It stops me dead in my tracks. I'm in space. I put the bike down on its two wheels, and I just stood there alone on the truck dock. I mean, it's four in the morning in a deserted part of the city. I'm three blocks from the river and the breeze is coming right off the water. Maybe it felt like floating because of the elevation of the truck dock above the street. My street is still cobblestones, you know, so with the streetlight down at the corner their bumpy tops are lit, and there are all these shadows between them so they look like stepping stones in black water. Or black nothingness. The light was really interesting, somehow crystal clear, with the contrasting shadows. It's hard to describe."

"You're doing a good job. It almost sounds like a dream."

"It was like that, except it was more real than what had been going on inside. No, not more real, but while I was inside it never would have occurred to me that I was three blocks from the river."

"It's like your insomnia, isn't it? You get stuck inside it, and forget, or forget how to get to, what's outside."

"I suppose. That fits. The trick is how to remember to get out."

"It doesn't work by trying. You can't will yourself to fall asleep."*

"And it's not just my insomnia, either. It's also like the other day, that session where I'd gotten all frustrated biking round the park, and then felt that puff—that's funny, there's the word—I felt that puff of affection towards you."

"It is like that. You're right. It's like turning your attention away from whatever starts to become all-consuming."

"Or just letting your attention turn itself away. There on the dock it wasn't like I had to do anything. Puff, and my eyes opened. There I was. Actually, after awhile I carried my bike the few steps down to the street and started cycling towards the river. I always go slow on my street because of the cobblestones—due deference to the perineum, I say—but I kept going slow even when I got to asphalt. I took the bike path downriver for awhile, looking at the lights and the tugboats and the water. And the wind. Of course, on the bike I make wind. It's like I can keep the wind with me. I didn't get into the "Drive on, driver!" mode, which I realize I'm in so much of the time. I just ambled, wandering really, round among all those little streets between the old skyscrapers. It's really neat down there at night, the streets empty, no one about except for the odd cop car or the occasional construction crew jackhammering away."

"You let yourself go."

"I guess I did. I did. I wasn't really thinking about anything."

"So let's see. With the insomnia you're chained to your thoughts, while with this wandering, you're unchained? You're still choosing, but it's different. You're free to go where you like?"

"Umh. When it started to get light I went down to the tip of the island and sat on one of those benches overlooking the harbor. At first I didn't like when it began to get full because I was missing the emptiness of the night. There started to be more people—pedestrian traffic and delivery trucks and the first ferry boats and helicopters. For some reason all these helicopters start up at dawn. But then it was dawn, the rosy-fingered real thing right out of the history books. I guess it's out of Homer, isn't it? I waited until I could see sky between the big ball of the sun and the horizon, and then I pedaled home and went to bed and slept like a baby until noon."

"Any dreams?"

"That's a joke, right? Enough material already, Doctor, what with my nocturnal adventure. No dreams, at least that I remember. Besides, babies don't dream, do they?"

"Actually, I think they do."

"Well, this baby didn't. It's funny, just now this matter-of-fact thought comes to me, 'You're no baby.' Maybe I'm more of a grown-up than I've thought."

"Maybe so."

"Well . . . So I woke up and ate and went down through Francesco's—actually I stopped on the stairs and went back up to get a light bulb to change on the landing. Francesco nods about how he really should clean up the stairway but I can tell I shouldn't hold my breath. Anyway he let me out onto the fire escape and I went up and razored open my windows. Now I have air."

"Room to breathe."

"I hope. I resisted my usual temptation to battle the automobiles on my way here, which is why I was a few minutes late."

"I prefer that you arrive in one piece."

"So do I. One piece, and a more peaceful piece. A more peaceful piece. Get it?"

"Unfortunately."

"It is true, though. I've got to remember wherever I am that I'm just three blocks from the river."

"Or remember to make your own wind, and that you can go where you like."

"Yes . . . Well, it must be time?"

"We still have a few minutes."

"And usually my internalized digital clock is so precise, emitting these piercing signals that it's time to hurry along to the next time when it'll be time to hurry along to the next time . . . Well . . . I really don't have to fill up the time, do I? I can just lie here?"

"That's right. It's up to you. It's your time. You can just lie there."

"So be it. Until it's time to shove along to work. Another day—rather another stimulating evening shift at the word processor—and another fifty cents . . ."

"Okay, our time is up."
"Next time, I'll be here on time."
"Take your time."
*"Let me out of here."**

3.

CONSCIOUSNESS

IN THE FIFTH GRADE of elementary school our science textbook told us not to sleep on our left sides. Since your heart is on your left side, it cautioned, adding the extra weight from your right side on top of your heart over the years could only add stress and shorten your life. It took me years to disbelieve this nostrum. The book also told us we had five senses, and I was at that age (I may be approaching it again) when listing all five for a test could pose a problem. The problem sprang from trying to remember what was in the book, rather than paying attention to what was in front of my nose. My nose: there's one; plus eyes, ears, tongue, and most acutely for touch, fingers, though another haptic appendage would soon assume prominence.

When I do pay attention to what is in front of my nose, the division of the senses is not so cut and dry. Was I the teacher's volunteer who ate an apple while smelling an onion? I should hope I had more sense. Do the peach-hued walls of a fancy restaurant make me hungry? I don't know how to tell. But if they do, surely the effect is less physiologic than associational. It's not that peach paint makes me salivate; it's that peachiness reminds me, if only subliminally, of a long-ago walk in a California peach grove where the peaches were falling like ripe scent bombs from the trees and to pick one up and eat it, warm and ready, bursting in the mouth, dripping down the chin, defined peachiness forevermore. Let's eat.

Rather, let's consider what makes these associations. That's what my science book left out. What pays attention to the senses is consciousness.

In Buddhist psychophysiology, as in ancient Indian, consciousness is the sixth sense. It is not some spooky sixth sense that raises hairs on the back of the neck upon the approach of the occult. It is ordinary consciousness, the roving mind's eye of attention. It pays attention to and coordinates the other senses, though at times, of course, consciousness seems just the facilitating servant of their appetites. Gorge now; wonder why later.

Just as one can be more or less involved in the moment with hearing or smelling or touching, one can be more or less conscious, somewhere along a range from hypervigilant arousal to dormancy. What uniquely marks consciousness, however, is that while it is in the moment, it is not exclusively of the moment. Consciousness can be conscious of itself; indeed, a self is someone aware of being conscious, that is, of being a being. There is no human monopoly on this. Any creature conscious enough to avoid being eaten by another one shows some measure of self-awareness. The human measure, of course, is not just consciousness of sensory experience, but of memories and anticipations, stories and explanations, worlds of subjectivity and objectivity and the intimate knowing of another self that reveals oneself anew. And all of these jostle for attention each moment in each one of us. Consciousness earmarks, if you hear me aright, our human being.

Then why was consciousness left out of my fifth-grade textbook? Because the study of consciousness was deemed, by and large during the last century in the West, unscientific. Science (at least *that* sort of science) strives to grab and hold and measure and test. Something so elusive as a state of being is hard enough to define, yet alone grab hold of. By the time I got to college the psychology department had been taken over by Stimulus and Response. Whatever it was that felt the stimulus and made the response was safely consigned to a black box that need never be opened.

Only psychoanalysis pried open the lid of that box, but it did so with the scientific pretensions necessary for some degree of academic legitimacy. The panoply of being could be fed into a reductionistic meat-grinder out of which came a few basic drives (sex and aggression), a few inevitable developmental complexes (mother-lusty Œdipus forfends castration), and a diagnostically interesting array of psychopathological categories in which to pigeonhole the suffering swarms of the earth. Nonetheless, with the lid of the sarcophagus ajar, psychoanalysis encountered the lambent will-o'-the-wisp of consciousness, the mystery of being. When the psychopharmacologists dethroned the psychoanalysts in psychiatry departments far and wide only a few decades ago, psychoanalysis was freed to return to its central philosophical concern: how is it, what is it, who is it, I am? The questions are not airy abstractions; they inform the repeated attention to the minutiae of consciousness that occurs session after session in every consulting room.

Science had made consciousness no matter. The decades shuffle past, the pendulum swings. Now of scientific concern is how matter makes mind. Recent developments in the field of neurology lend themselves to an understanding not only of psychoanalytic change, but also, as we shall see, to an understanding of Buddhist explanations of self and mindfulness.

I do not propose to digress into neurology here, but instead to seize on one informed speculation about how the brain underpins the mind: the "dynamic core hypothesis."* The dynamic core is not a place in the brain, but a process generated among neurons. It is a complicated process, given that there are 30 billion neurons with a million billion connections between them allowing for $10^{1,000,000}$ possible neural circuits. This compares to the measly 10^{79} particles in the known universe (give or take a handful). In such a complex system as the brain, and quite in line with mathematical complexity theory, repeating patterns of neuronal firing tend to establish themselves: order arises out of chaos. The patterns are not dependent on particular neurons, which may be activated or not, join in or drop out.

I once went to a rug factory outside Kathmandu, where a chant hung hovering in the air of the wool-spinning loft. At first I thought it came over loudspeakers, but as I looked around I realized the Tibetan spinners were more and less chanting. A nearby fellow had stopped and was trying to sell me trinkets; others were involved sporadically in occasional conversations; people would variously drop out of the chanting and then resume it. Meanwhile the chant itself hung clear as a bell in the air.

Just so with the neuronal patterning. Memories are patterns. The present is a "remembered present" since it is understood against fluctuating resonances of the past. I remember what is in order to construct reality anew. Simpler patterns give rise to more complex patterns, which in turn complexify. Some patterns are unconscious, though they may affect the whole. Indeed, everything, according to this hypothesis, affects everything (to greater and lesser degrees) because all neuronal activity is interrelated. The analogy is to coupled springs. Imagine a roomful of bedsprings, all tangled and in tension with one another. The most tangled central cluster is the dynamic core. A twang to one of its springs quickly sets them all humming, while a twang to an incidental spring off at the corner of the room is barely audible.

The dynamic core, as I understand it, is a neurological explanation of my fluctuating but self-sustaining consciousness, my orb of awareness constituted by patterns past and present and requiring, like an old house, constant maintenance. The dynamic core enlists my various subselves in a joint meeting so that they can agree to a proclamation through my mouth of what "I" think. The dynamic core is an enormously complex process of self-sustaining patterning. Its culminating pattern is self, unique in each moment but felt as that same old ongoing "me."

The psychoanalytic process, by analogy, works at the level of twanging key bedsprings—that is, homing in on self-generating patterns and by activating them in a novel way (as objects of analysis) freeing them to change. Just as self is a recurrent patterning, so is character,* and so is psychopathology. Change requires a kind of surrender, a letting go of old habitual patterning. The psychoanalytic process is top down, using consciousness to alter itself, rather than resorting to the bottom-up use of drugs or brain surgery. Tops down, bottoms up, they are all interconnected. Thoughts affect the physiology of the brain, as well as the other way around.

And what of the "process," so to speak, of Buddhism, the path to enlightenment? Two features stand out. One is that the contemporary "dynamic core hypothesis" is quite similar to the Buddhist understanding of self that has endured for two and a half thousand years. The second is that the neurological hypothesis culminates in self, while Buddhist psychology transcends it. For neurology, an explanation of how brain processes produce experience of me-in-the-moment is sufficient. For Buddhism, the experience of me-in-the-moment is a starting place for the deeper exploration of experience.

In Buddhism, too, the self emerges from the interaction of complex underlying patterns.* The five senses and consciousness, the sixth, comprise modes in which sensation constantly arises and passes away. Every moment of experience requires an organ of perception, an object of perception, and an admixture of consciousness. Without some degree of consciousness the organ cannot be aware of the object. The mind is the organ of consciousness, and is able to take for objects of perception its own contents. All experience is accordingly triangulated between the perceiving organ, the perceived object, and awareness thereof. The self arises through this triangulation of subsidiary aggregates. Awareness of perceiving and perceived generates a perceiver. Like a swirl of smoke over fire, self simply appears.

It is not that self is an illusion. Self *is,* but it is without any intrinsic existence beyond the temporary conditions that give it rise. The function of self is to provide continuity to experience, which boils down to perpetuating self. It does this marvelously well, given the underlying complexities.

The self digests experience to preserve itself. The metaphor applies to life. Those first plankton in their soupy prehistoric sea photosynthetically digested sunlight, in a sense, to prolong and preserve their cells with the stored energy of carbohydrates (if I remember well my textbook). The self-serving amalgamation of complexity compounds larger organisms to consume those carbohydrates, and then to consume each other, the winners better and better able (by Darwinian selection) to digest greater complexities of variation and deprivation into the ongoing species of themselves. Consciousness is nascent in the effort to recognize what to eat, and how not to be eaten.

And so here am I, not at the pinnacle of evolution but certainly an aspect of it. I digest moment by moment my experience, thinking to preserve my ongoingness. Some of what I digest I turn into words, and proffer them to you as a nourishing snack, a tidbit, if you like, around which you may wrap yourself the better to recognize yourself in relation to it at a later date. Let's eat. (The peaches were insufficient.)

That's as far as I get with myself. Self munches along, tending to provide more of the same. The problem is, the peaches are always insufficient. Each meal is just a temporary stopgap forestalling the void of hunger. My form will be emptiness. My glorious self, my thoughts and hopes, my valued mementos, achievements and shames, all poof! And then where am I? No I, no where. Sickness, aging, and death triangulate their crosshairs without fail. The worms will eat my neurons. Am I a singing fool tripping along towards dusty death?

The Buddha, I imagine, would answer, "Yes." I am a fool to the extent that I believe "I" am all I've got. Yet how could it be otherwise, when consciousness seems always to drag this epiphenomenon of "I" in its wake? When "I" seem so embedded in body and brain?

This is where the Buddha's answer gets interesting: transcend self.

First let's review. Culminating years of effort, he gets enlightened under the bodhi tree. At first he thinks no one could possibly understand what he has ascertained, but then he decides to go to Deer Park to tell his former cronies. With stupendous effect, in that they become enlightened, he delivers the Four Noble Truths: that life entails suffering, that the source of suffering is desire, that there is attainable cessation of desire, and that attainment can be approached via the Eightfold Path. Buddhism in a nutshell.

The nut is rather more complicated. Apart from two-plus millenia of scholarship and schism, the originary sutras themselves are extensive. Having framed the basic understanding of Buddhism with the Four Noble Truths, the Buddha went on to detail thirty-seven aspects of the path to enlightenment,* in which list the *eightfold path* covers steps twenty-three to thirty. It ends with *seven branches of enlightenment* (such as right equanimity); prior to the path are the *five powers* derived from the *five faculties* (e.g., faith, joyous effort), in turn developed from the *four supernatural feats* (feats of extraordinary single-pointed concentration) ensuing practice of the *four correct endeavors* (abandoning negative and enhancing positive acts). Most relevant here, however, are the *four foundations of mindfulness* with which the list begins.

The foundations are mindfulness of the body, mindfulness of feelings, mindfulness of the mind, and mindfulness of phenomena.

What is mindfulness?* Strictly speaking, it is not consciousness at all.

Mindfulness is a quality of mind that can be developed through meditation, but unlike consciousness, it may or may not be present at any given moment of awareness. One can be happily fantasizing, plotting revenge, dividing the restaurant bill, or carrying on a conversation, all with no mindfulness at all. Mindfulness is not a mode of consciousness, but rather a relational formation among the modal inputs of experience. It is a construction of the moment, arising and passing away like all else, but a construction that can become habitual with practice over time. Moments of mindfulness may arise spontaneously, but are typically momentary. Established mindfulness is present not just to the moment, but to moments in series. To mindfulness, the content of consciousness is almost incidental, whether it be pleasurable or painful, loving or hateful. The intention of mindfulness is simply to be present with whatever consciousness presents, to witness its arising and its passing away.

What is mindfulness? It is kin, I believe, to what Freud described as the "evenly suspended attention"* of psychoanalysis. Freud enjoined the analyst when listening to a patient to drop preconceived assumptions and expectations, to open non-judgmentally to the associational flow. Similarly, if the patient is "free-associating," a flitting remove from the adhesiveness of passing thoughts is assumed. Free association is not easy; rather it is an accomplishment. An old psychoanalytic joke has it that when the patient can finally free associate, the analysis is over.

This is a key feature of the technique of psychoanalysis: to observe the interaction while participating in it, to step back and reflect even as events whirr along. There is a back and forth motion, from being in the rush of things to finding oneself apart from the rush of things, from immersion to reflection. It's not that the motion is regular or easy to manage, but the psychoanalytic set-up implies that there is room for motion, that is, room to step aside from the normative and habitual patterns of living that brought the patient to analysis in the first place. In a way, analyst and analysand periodically step back into mindfulness in order to see what's going on, before what's going on again rises like the flood tide to sweep them along.

The French author Alphonse Daudet* considered himself cursed from youth with being *homo duplex.* When he was sixteen and his father rushed in with the news of his brother's death—"He's dead! He's dead!"—his "first Me" burst into tears, while his "second Me" thought what a terrific impression such a shout would make as a piece of theatre. His first Me grappled with the struggles of his life, while the second Me, always there, never drunk, tearful, or sleepy, simply watched with unmoving neutrality, seeing into things. Had that second Me been less a thinker, and more just an observer of that thought about a *coup de théâtre,* that second Me might well match mindfulness.

From existential psychoanalysis comes a notion of two realms of the will.* The first realm comprises what we think of as conscious choice: whether we will have the soup or the salad, what we will do with a free afternoon. The second realm deals less with doing than with being, with finding how we are. Sleepy? Hungry? Happy? In the second realm, one does not so much will an action as find oneself willing to enter into the nature of ongoing experience. The element of mindfulness lies in allowing to arise what will arise.

Similarly, there is the argument that people come for analysis when they have forgotten how to forget.* In other words, they become stuck with and hindered by their obsessions, fears, and foibles. They cannot forget what has been or cease dreading what might yet be. Forgetting, in this context, means living in such a way as to allow to come up what comes up, to allow what passes away to pass away. Living in such a way is living with mindfulness.

Those who have forgotten how to forget, from a Buddhist perspective, are embroiled with the organ of the mind. This is not just a proclivity to attend to consciousness more than other qualities of experience; it is more an obsession with self, an egomania. I am preoccupied with what is happening to me in my world and your job is to say what you think about me. The self so exaggeratedly preoccupied with its own continuity becomes self-centered, self-serving, and selfish, if not tyrannical, abusive, and megalomaniacal. What can be done?

The psychoanalyst sees years of work ahead. For that matter, so does the Buddhist. The antidote is mindfulness.

Along the Buddhist path, assuming that our egoist is enough self-aware to realize something must be done about unsatisfactory patterns of living, he or she may begin with the first foundation: mindfulness of the body. The meditative approach is to sit regularly for a given period of time and to turn the attention to a particular aspect of the body, say, the breath. Such close concentration rapidly reveals the typical distracted hubbub clamoring in the mind. Before one knows it, one is railroaded along with the clickety-clack thoughts, or enticed by the pleasant fantasies, or wrenched by the old agonies. The breath is quite forgotten. One notices the breath is quite forgotten, attempts not to board the train of self-flagellating thoughts about personal failure as a meditator, attempts simply, instead, to return the attention to the breath. Again the attention wanders, again the attention returns to the breath. This is killing my back; my ankles are falling asleep. Again, the breath. How long has this been? Isn't the time up? Again, the breath, shivering hairs in the nostrils. What is it about my nose? Again, the breath. Time's up.

With repetition and continued effort at concentration, it gets easier. Part of the inducement to continue the practice may well be the opportunity to escape, if only for a little, the mental cabin in which one finds oneself stir-crazy.

Likewise, for psychoanalysis, typically begun with little instruction and little direction, the methodically regular visits to the consulting room can become a kind of time out, variously an opportunity to pause for an "Up periscope!" on life, or to dump and leave anxieties, or to break the routine. The interpersonal pull is to wonder, if only vaguely, how one appears in the eye of the other. Am I lecturing, preening before, supplicating, or seducing my analyst? Such questions can lead toward mindfulness. The analyst is there as the unblinking observer (so it might seem), modeling a mindful regard of oneself.

The second foundation is mindfulness of feeling. This is not the sense of touch, but the aggregate affective tone which accompanies moment by moment experience. Feeling ranges from positive to neutral to negative, and like everything else, changes moment by moment, arising and passing away. The positive feelings come, I want to cling; the negative, to avoid; the neutral, perhaps to sleep. But just as I concentrated on letting the thoughts go to return to my breath, so I intend to let the feelings pass, neither clinging nor thrusting away. It takes practice.

And in analysis, the forgotten feelings are often addressed, since it is so easy to forget, or to prefer to forget, one feels anything out of the ordinary at all. How were you feeling then, when so-and-so made that comment? When such-and-such happened in your dream? How were you feeling just now, when you paused before you spoke? How might I be feeling, to hear you say that? What does it mean, when you look away? It's curious, when you feel nothing at all.

The third foundation is mindfulness of mind. The intention is not to become aware of every passing mental content, but to become aware of the nature of the organ of the mind itself. Does it tend to react with aversion or hatred? With lust or greed? With hapless confusion or denial? Where the first foundation focused on the content of a physical sensation, and the second foundation focused on the textured nuances of feeling, the third foundation proposes attention to the overall quality of mind.

Analytically, I believe, this translates into work on character. Character is a shorthand description of the way one comports oneself in the world—what one is like, how one seems to others. Character may be that global flag that tells us to avoid certain others at a party, or that, unseen as it flutters overhead, tells certain others to avoid us. Character can reveal such deep-seated assumptions as that the world should take care of me, or that only cynical I am no fool, or that it's dog-eat-dog and I bite. Working free of such assumptions requires recognizing them, hence an element of mindfulness.

On extended examination, however, character is not so unitary, and what may well pop into being are various sub-selves. In some situations one may act and feel oneself to be, let's say, the fragile flower Mother strove to protect, while in other situations one is Uncle's athletic bruiser, or Auntie's intellectual. Such self-states and shifts between them are usually unconscious, unless brought to consciousness by the analytically contrived provision of room for quiet observation.

And character and self-states are but one side of the equation. Going along with who I take myself to be is, concordantly, who I take you to be. Freud called this aspect of things the "transference," that is, the carrying over from the past and application to the present of a set of expectations as to who the other person (in particular, the analyst) is. Analysis of the transference is often considered the hallmark of psychoanalytic psychotherapy. The situation grows more complicated with the recognition of multiple self-states and correspondingly multiple self-state responses in the analyst, plus the fact that the patient is not the Stimulus and analyst the Response because each in interaction perpetually stimulates and responds to the other. These complications are part of the reason analytic treatment is typically a matter of years. When it works, the years may tease out the no longer applicable premise that one is, say, a fragile flower the other will surely either water or pluck. One becomes free to live differently.

One forgets, unmindfully, that one looks at the world through a set of mental spectacles, adopted because of circumstances and personal situations gone by. Things change. One might see more clearly without them.

The fourth foundation is mindfulness of mental phenomena. This is not attention's return to a round-the-mulberry-bush chasing of chattering thoughts, because attention is presumably more practiced and concentrated through meditation on the first three foundations. The fourth foundation entails regarding mental contents with discernment, against the template of the other thirty-three aspects of the path to enlightenment. Mental phenomena can be seen, for example, in terms of their positive or negative karmic consequences. Each thought, each action, has consequences, both for oneself and for others, so the responsibility to live well alters the world. You must mind what you do. The goal is not mindfulness as an end in itself, but as a means to know how better to live—how, ultimately, to reach the wisdom of enlightenment.

Psychoanalysis lays no claim to wisdom. Or does it? In one way the paths of Buddhism and psychoanalysis seem to diverge at the fourth foundation. Psychoanalysis (certain critics aside) is not, after all, a religion. It has no cosmology, no explicit series of steps to take towards a defined (even if mystically incomprehensible) end, no code of moral behavior to prescribe. Its goals are earth-bound—how to live in the world now with less suffering—rather than linked to a soteriology of salvation. In theory and in practice it espouses no theology, no spiritual necessities. It does none of these things—explicitly.

If psychoanalysis is not a religion, and not a science, then what is it? Psychoanalysis is a way of paying attention to the flow of consciousness. And the flow is not just within oneself, but between oneself and another. It is a way to lift one's nose (again, the nose) from the grindstone of doing the next thing, chasing the next thought, to find some wider perspective, some deeper understanding. Accordingly its goal, like that of the fourth foundation, is to witness the flow of mental phenomena with discernment. Its goal is an alteration in one's way of being.

And what is discernment? Buddhism is explicit about this, and its teachings can guide a lifetime of study and practice towards a more enlightened way of being. Yet that way of being is also earth-bound, affecting how to live in the world now with less suffering. It is like the story of the Zen monk who, when asked how enlightenment had changed him, replied, "Before I was enlightened, I ate, I drank, I slept. After I was enlightened, I ate, I drank, I slept." Discernment entails how one regards the ordinary. Mindfulness is a stance of regard, including how one regards one's "self."

To the extent that the "analytic attitude"* mirrors a stance of mindfulness, those same discerning considerations that follow explicitly from mindfulness in Buddhism, follow implicitly from mindfulness in psychoanalysis. Changing one's way of being necessarily entails changing not just symptomatically, not just psychologically, but as well ethically, interpersonally, and spiritually, even if those dimensions of being remain latent and undiscussed.

For example, let us imagine a patient, say his name is Ebenezer, who despite the accumulation of wealth that was supposed to make him happy, still feels something is awry—particularly because of some walloping bad dreams. He reluctantly decides to come for analysis, and begins his treatment with a litany of complaints about the fee. In due course, that concern could lead to reflection about what money means to him, how it came to be, what he has been afraid of, what he has been grasping onto, what are his hopes, his fondest desires, what is his effect on those around him, how he is when he gloats and rubs gold coins against his palms, how he is when he shivers in bed from doing without an extra log on the fire, how he feels when he orders his clerk to work late, when he cheats, when he steals. What comes up in reflecting on all these things is necessarily a cold-eyed assessment of how he thinks, acts, and feels, and what consequences his thoughts, actions, and feelings lead to. In understanding why he holds so tight his wad of bills, he may find he no longer needs or wants to. And he no longer needs or wants to because he has begun to *discern* a better way of living. After all, he came to analysis to get better. When he started, getting better meant not having those bad dreams. By the time he finishes (on Christmas Day, special session) getting better means living by a different set of standards as to what is good and bad. His change is ethical, as well as change along so many other dimensions of being. He has reassessed the good, and altered his way of being accordingly. One could call the change psychoanalytic, or for that matter, Christian, Buddhist, Muslim, Jewish, or humanist. But Ebenezer lives with less suffering, and suffer less those around him.

My suggestion, then, is that in their approach to the exploration of consciousness, Buddhism and psychoanalysis share a similar strategy, though different means. The strategy is the development of mindfulness. There is not just one way to do this across the various schools of Buddhism, but "entering the stream" cannot neglect the thirty-seven aspects of the path to enlightenment. There is not just one prescribed way to develop that "analytic attitude" in psychoanalysis, nor, psychoanalysts being the cantankerous lot they are, is there general agreement that that's what psychoanalysis is all about. But I think so: there is in psychoanalysis mindfulness.

The Buddhist practitioner, entered on the path, encounters the three snarling dogs of greed, hatred, and ignorance. They appear in one's covetousness, gluttony, lust, spitefulness, arrogance, prejudice, complacency, avoidance, denial, and all the rest. The challenge is to turn these negativities and the consequences they ineluctably generate into beneficent positives.

Those snarling dogs don't bite only Buddhists. Each of us has been mauled. Each of us needs to get better. We begin through turning attention.

Good Day, Good Night

"So, I don't know what to talk about today. Nothing particularly comes to mind."

"Hmh."

"What do you think? Is there anything in particular I should be talking about at this point in analysis?"

"What matters?"

"Well, the old answering the question with a question technique. Though of course you're suggesting I get down to what matters. If I knew what mattered to talk about I wouldn't be asking you what to talk about, would I?"

"Hmh."

"You're not going to answer? This is helpful?"

"Perhaps. What do you want of me? Who do you want me to be?"

"Well, I . . . I guess I really don't want you to tell me what to talk about. Then I'd just be doing your assignment or pleasing you, something like that. So you toss the hot potato back to me."

"What about it is like a 'hot potato'?"

"Hot potato, let's see. Something you want to get rid of by tossing it to someone else. So what's 'hot' about not knowing what to talk about? Maybe . . . Maybe I just want to know that you're there to catch it, even if you do toss it back."

"I am here."

"That's what's hot. Is it? I mean, it's not just that you're here, but it's whether you're here for me. If I'm just an object of your technique, I might as well be some guinea pig in your maze. Actually, come to think of it, in a way that would be comforting. We'd each know what to do. You put me in at the beginning of this maze called 'Psychoanalysis' and watch, maybe timing it and taking notes, while I run around bumping my nose into various dead-ends until either I expire—get the picture, there I am on my little furry back, four legs stiff in the air, a little X across each fuzzy eyelid—or else I finally get some sense in my head and clamber out of the maze, maybe biting your finger as I escape."

"You've gotten to the hot stuff."

"Because it wouldn't be comforting just to give up and be a guinea pig. It's embarrassing, but I want to know that I actually do matter to you, and not just as another patient."

"How can you know that?"

"How? It's not so obvious. You can't just say that I matter because then you might just be saying it, like giving me what you think I need. How do I know it? It's a matter of trust, whether I can trust you or trust myself to know whether you actually are there for me . . . But you know, I think I really do trust it. Otherwise I wouldn't still be here. I'm not that dumb. I would've jumped up and left long ago, though hopefully without biting your finger along the way. I can doubt it or forget about it or just not pay attention, but when you come right down to it I feel like you have accepted me, or let me show you who I am. You actually may know me better than anyone else. Who else do I talk to like this? Nobody, not ever. Even with Karen, I mean we used to tell each other how we felt and stuff, and I did feel like I could be myself with her, but it always got down to wanting the other person to change, and neither of us could change the way the other wanted. So I'm too needy and she's too selfish and she breaks it off and I think seriously about tossing in the towel for good and end up coming to see you and a couple of years later here we are, still."

"Here we are, still. And between us?"

"*Well, I guess the needy part is different. I mean I did need you at the begin-ning, sort of like a shoulder to cry on, but I didn't want really to need you, like being dependent on you, because . . . because it would feel humiliating, like I can't manage my life on my own, and either I need this crutch of analysis to keep going or else I've been brainwashed into thinking I do. But the funny part now, at this point, is that I do need you but not in a needy way.*"

"*How's that?*"

"*Well, it's not like the analysis is a crutch. I could get along without it, but it's useful, like a tool to keep track of what's going on, or to keep stuff in per-spective. Or more than that, it's like a reminder that I can shift perspectives. Like when I used to beat myself up—not that I don't get into delivering judg-ments on myself now, but before we started talking about it I didn't even real-ize that that's what I was doing. I thought I was just facing facts about my worthlessness. It never occurred to me that I was also making an excuse so I wouldn't have to do anything about it but could just sit around and feel sorry for myself. And sit with that dash of self-righteousness about how nobly I was suffering. God, just thinking about it, sometimes I make myself sick. That's ironic. I was making myself sick but without realizing it, and at this point— on a good day—I can pull out of it and make myself some other way. Or at any rate, notice there's room for some other way to come along and then notice when it does. It's not like I can just reprogram the computer, 'Move from Square One to Square Two.' It's more like being able to remember when I'm in Square One that it's not the only show in town.*"

"*I take it today is a good day.*"

"*Well, now that you ask, I guess so. Yes, it is a good day, and I'm glad that you're there to ask and for me to tell you. Checking in on myself I realize I'm actually feeling all right, which reminds me on my way here—I was just tool-ing along, taking it easy—and I found myself humming, not quite sure of the tune, which then came to me, that old Shaker hymn, I think it is, "'Tis a joy to be simple, 'tis a joy to be free.' So I'm humming along and of course I thought wait 'til you get a load of this when I tell you about it.*"

"*Sounds good to me.*"

"*I don't know where it came from. Out o' the blue. Look, I'm smiling now, just remembering it.*"

"*You weren't thinking about anything in particular?*"

"No, it was just a bonus good feeling, sort of like that puff of wind the other week? I just found myself humming along, happy, no need to think about why. 'Don't look a gift horse in the mouth.' You know it wasn't until college that I learned that that means you're not supposed to offend whoever is giving you a horse by looking for cavities or signs of aging and stuff in the horse's mouth. As a kid I always thought why would anyone ever look in a horse's mouth anyway, just ride the horse like you're supposed to instead of doing something weird. I didn't know looking at the mouth is a usual thing in horsetrading or whatever, not that I know much more about horses now."

"And you were a weird kid."*

"That's a bit blunt, isn't it?"

"It still hurts?"

"Not the weirdness part. I mean, at this point I can look back on myself as a kid and almost take pride in having been different."

"But I was 'a bit blunt.' Something still hurts?"

"You know, it's not the being weird. It's like I'm super-sensitive to—to whether you might be rejecting me."

"Shades of Dad?"

"Sure. Always too busy with important work to notice unimportant me. I had to hide how weird I felt to hope for any attention from him at all."

"Maybe his very lack of attention made you feel weird?"

"That was only part of it. God, if the other boys had ever found out I was doing embroidery for a hobby! At least Mom could keep a secret."

"And she was a good teacher."

"Let's see, French knot, chain stitch, I can't remember all the names. But I bet I could still manage a little flower garden, with daisies and irises and a big sheltering tree."

"You're smiling again."

"You know, that is a good memory of my mother. It was all right by her if I wanted to embroider doilies. So Dad would be off on some business trip and she and I would sit at the dining room table after dinner with all the embroidery hoops and pretty colored thread and she'd show me stitches and we'd sew away . . . I wonder if she'd wished I'd been a girl?"

"Any guesses?"

"I don't suppose so. I mean—particularly with the way she was while she was *dying, knitting me that sweater—I think she basically accepted me the way I was. Even if she wished she had had a daughter, that didn't mean she didn't want to have me, or that I was supposed to try to be a girl. That would really have been a problem. Like my experimenting in high school to find out if I was gay, with all the shame. I don't think she would have cared. As far as she was concerned I could just be me, a boy who liked to sit with her at the dining room table and learn embroidery. That was just fine. It could just look a little weird from the outside."*

"As it did to your father."

"Unfortunately. But now I don't really have to care what it looked like to him, do I? I know what it looks like to me."

"You can be weird and all right."

"Lo and behold. Though you know he still doesn't get me. When he comes to town and invites me to his Club for those lunches, I feel duty-bound to go despite how excruciating it is to sit there with him. I mean if I don't fill up the time regaling him with stories it's like there's nothing between us but the clink-clink of the silverware on the china and I'm just dying for the meal to end. And when I do tell him little stories about what's going on in my life— 'Not a lot going on in my life, Dad. I learned a new formatting technique at the law firm.'— it's like he's listening politely but still privately thinking, 'What a weirdo!' And despite getting a handle on all this in here I just can't face trying really to talk to him about any of this."

"What do you imagine it'd be like?"

"Let's see. If I said . . . what would I say? 'Do you love me?' That would blow him out of the water. No, the problem is it wouldn't blow him out of the water. He'd say, 'Of course,' and get all tight-lipped and I'd have this huge sinking feeling."

"Tell me more about that feeling."

"It's the falling down feeling again, isn't it? I know: it's like I've disappointed him again even by asking the question. I'm not supposed to ask, 'Do you love me?' or anything like that because that's off limits and I'm perpetually disappointing him by not living according to his limits. Which enrages me, too, of course."

"If I understand this right, getting enraged doesn't free you because part of you still believes he's right? You still carry around the feeling that fundamentally you are a disappointment?"*

"Well, we're trying to create some room for me to work out of that one, aren't we?"

"Yes, that seems right. And you're finding the room, too, aren't you? Like today, when it's 'a joy to be simple, a joy to be free.' You're remembering it's a good day."

"You know, when I think about Dad today I actually feel less angry than sorry for him. He's so buttoned up and scared, though that's the last way he'd think of himself. He thinks of himself as confident and cultured and appropriately reserved, like some goddam English gentleman. 'Let's not talk about anything messy, or anything I—that means me, as far as he's concerned—might be interested in, but instead let's go have some private æsthetic orgasm at the concert hall.' You know, when I was eight or nine he took me to my first concert. So he's sitting there closing his eyes at the exquisiteness of some diminuendo, while I'm writhing around with ants in my pants. We had to leave at intermission, my hand in his like a vise-grip, tears streaming down my face, and he wouldn't say a thing. It would have been better if he'd yelled at me, but instead it was like this silent condemnation I could never hope to do anything about. At least that's the way it feels now. Then all I knew was I felt awful. Christ, I was nine years old! What did he expect?"

"And it's like a miniature repetition, when you can barely sit still through lunch with him."

"Exactly."

"What would it be like to talk with him about your memory of that concert?"

"You know, you might be onto something there. I just had the thought that he'd be squirming in his seat instead of me. Not that I really want him to squirm—though that'd be sort of fun—but it could be like touching base on the fact that, 'Gee Dad, we really have shared a life together. Do you remember when I was nine and you took me to the concert? What was it like for you? . . . I really would like to know' . . . You know, I think I might actually ask him next time he flies through town . . . You know, as I think about it, what I'd actually like to ask him?"

"What?"

"About Mom. Whether he thinks about her much, or misses her. I mean, from the way we've discussed it, it doesn't seem like it was a close marriage, to put it mildly, with him traveling so much and Mom essentially waiting around."

"'Waiting around' puts the embroidery in different light. Was it like she was waiting for him to come home for her life to begin?"

"Sure. I mean it wasn't like she had a big social life or her own work or anything."

"She had you."

"She had me. And I had her, sure. Starts to sound a bit much, doesn't it?"

"How do you mean?"

"Well, she's waiting around for a husband who ignores her when he is around, and I'm there like her sole companion, and that's it. That's her life."

"And yours, too? Waiting around with her?"

"Well, I had school and I did have friends to do stuff with plus all those various afterschool lessons and everything. But Mom was home. I mean, she was the one I came home to."

"I imagine her waiting around for you, too."

"Jesus, she must've been so depressed. Otherwise, why wouldn't she have gone out and done something?"

"Maybe it's like you've been waiting around, the past few years?"*

"Huh! There's something to that. It is like I've been marching in place. And it's a really familiar feeling, because of Mom. You know, it's almost like waiting around brings her back to me, or makes me closer to her in some weird way."

"Another bit of weirdness."

"Which I think I'm better off without . . . You know, I don't just miss her and feel sorry for her, I also miss what she didn't give me. I mean it makes me angry that all she'd do was wait around."

"She was too passive."

"Yeah, she had a streak of that. She made a kind of cocoon for me, but couldn't help me get out of it. Except by dying. And Dad forces me out. You know, I think he clammed up even more after she died. It was like he was properly mournful and observed the proprieties and then got back to business as usual, but it changed him more than that. I think of him as seeming old from that point. I remember when I got back from my first semester at boarding school I hadn't seen him for three months and when I first saw him at the top of the stairs how old he looked."

"How'd you feel?"

"Well, I was still pissed off at having been shipped off to school and I was ready to give him grief—"

"That's an interesting way to put it: 'give him grief.'"

"Hmh. It was like I was still grieving and he seemed done, which I resented. But when I saw him looking old? It scared me. I thought, 'What if he dies, too?'"

"You realized you needed him?"

"From the way I see it now, it isn't just that I needed him. It's that despite how aloof he is and how hurtful his criticism can be he does still matter to me. Underneath everything, I do love him. If I didn't, it wouldn't be so upsetting. And so every time, even though it's just lunch, never dinner not to mention a little vacation or something, every time I do accept his invitation to lunch."

"So you're there for him?"

"I guess I am. And I guess he is for me, too, as well as he can manage, in his own half-assed way. It does make me less angry at him, thinking of it like this. Like next time when we meet, maybe I can get him to stroll down memory lane a bit. Maybe I can get him to open up, instead of feeling like it's always my job to fill the silence. After all, he's got to have stories, too. We've even got stories together."

"It's a different stance. It's like you're reaching out for him rather than feeling helpless and boxed in."

"That sounds about right . . . That's it . . . Well, talk about silence . . ."

"Are you helpless and boxed in?"

"No, that's not it at all. I'm just letting Dad go, drifting a bit . . . Shall I get you to tell me some stories?"

"What sorts of stories do you imagine I—"

"I know, I know. It's about my stories, not yours. It's funny how little I know about you when I also know you so well."

"There are different sorts of knowing."*

"That's for sure . . . Well . . ."

" . . ."

"Oh, I didn't tell you. I do have a story. I met someone last night."

"Last night?"

"Yeah, I took another insomnia ride—actually, you know, my sleep has been getting much better. I've mostly been sleeping right through. But last night I woke up in the middle of the night and it felt like this golden opportunity. It was a beautiful night. Did you get out?"

"Not last night."

"See what you miss by not being weird?"

*"Do you think I'm learning?"**

"There's definite progress. But last night: I woke up and pedaled around and stopped at that plaza by the Fey Street building. Do you know it?"

"No, I don't think I do."

"Well it's that skyscraper done in the '60s, I imagine, with neon tunnels leading to the lobby and sort of whimsical colorful neon touches here and there on the façade."

"I think I have seen it."

"Do you remember the clock?"

"No."

"This'll take some explaining. It doesn't even look like a clock. There's like this big billboard set over the plaza, only it's a big grid of glass squares with five rows of twelve squares each?"

"All right. A big wall of glass squares."

"Only they're numbered from one to sixty and they light up. The one that glows red tells the hour. There's one glowing blue that tells the minute. Meanwhile, the squares flash white second by second."

"Okay."

"So you watch the white seconds march along from one until sixty when the blue square moves along a notch to mark the next minute. Got it?"

"I think so. I'm waiting for you to meet someone?"

"Patience! These things take time!"

"Like psychoanalysis?"

"We're almost there. When the blue hits sixty it makes the red hour change, but the blue disappears for a minute, until it's a minute past the hour and it lights up blue in the number one square. Understand?"

"Red's the hour, blue's the minute, white's the second."

"And they're all changing with the seconds charging along. Really, the whole thing is hypnotic, mostly because it's so big but also because it takes awhile at first to figure out the thing is a clock."

"Some clock."

"So I'm down there sitting on the bike one foot on a bench thinking now what happens when it's 3:03:03, which it almost is. I could sort of tell because when the red and the blue want to light up the same square, the red comes from

the top and the blue from the bottom. Then when the white second comes marching along at 3:03:03, the whole square flashes super white, like a flash bulb going off. Cheap thrills, huh?"

"For this I should have stayed up?"

"But the thing is, just as 3:03:03 happens I notice out of the corner of my eye that there's another person. And she's also on a bike about thirty feet away watching the clock."

"What timing."

"So without thinking I call out to her, 'Did you see that?' meaning the white flash, of course. But she must not have seen me so she's alarmed and starts to pedal away—there's no one around and this is the middle of the night in a deserted plaza, so I can understand it—but I say 'Wait a minute!' in some such way that she stops and looks at me. I was smiling away and made some stupid joke about how we had a minute, so she must've thought anyone who can make such a stupid joke can't be all that threatening. She stopped and we had this conversation, calling across this no-man's-land safe distance between us. Turns out she's a baker—that's why she's out at that hour, just finished putting her croissants in for something called 'proofing' before they're baked in the morning—and she bicycles because it's impossible to get a cab at that hour and she was the only one with a pencil so she took my number and said it'd be fun to go biking sometime. Her name is Grace.* She'll call. You know, I really think she will call. It was so cool and unusual meeting in the middle of the night like that."

"You're attacted to her?"

"You bet. She was pretty with this thick curly hair and bright eyes."

"And you had nothing to talk about today?"

"I guess I didn't want to look a gift horse in the mouth."

"That's our time."

"I know."

4.

MYSTERIES BETWEEN

WHAT IS IT, TO BE BETWEEN? At first, I don't think of myself as being between anything. Simply, I am. But then between creeps in. I am between what I am not.

> In a field
> I am
> the absence of field.
> This is always the case.
> Wherever I am,
> I am
> what is missing . . .*

What is missing is what is between. I come between things. I am a nexus, the crossing point of a multiplicity of betweens. I find myself between birth and death, dawn and dusk, between memory and expectation, between this very word and the word to come. I even find myself, if only I open to it, not by my solitary self, but somewhere between you and me.

How we are when we are with each other arises from who we are through being with each other. We are not separate endpoints, a discrete you and a discrete me, because each of us is different, changed, in regard of the other. Who I am as a separate person is not who I am with you in mind. Through extending ourselves towards each other, each of us becomes a go-between. Like a cable-car funicular dangling among mountaintops, who I am goes somewhere between us. I have a choice, as do you, even because having no choice is something one chooses. I can choose to close down, back off, try to make you a mere object in the world, the same as all those others; I can open, risk meeting, ease forward, lose my separate self to find myself anew in your eyes and in my own. We have a choice as to whether we allow our meeting to matter. Meetings that matter change us.

So let us see, in this chapter, if we can swing between two ideas. By the one idea, I find myself as something passively given, present like flotsam in the flow of experience; by the other idea, I am self-chosen, a swimmer actively altering experience to sustain myself anew. The one idea is of oneself as a resultant experiential nexus, a confluent tangle at the center of the associational matrix of what comes to mind all by itself; the other idea, complementarily, is of oneself as a chooser, minding what comes to mind, consciously or not affecting, moreover effecting the world, by attention and action—and in particular by attention to, and action towards, one another. Along particular lines of association, via unseen lines overhead, the one idea leads naturally to the other.

Come into the funicular's windowed car. The doors safely shut, the cable grips overhead, we begin to sway and rise away through mountain mists and crystal air, into the between.

Begin where you are, at the nexus, the point between. Between what?

Between, in the macrocosm, here and there, between then and when, suspended, dangling, in space and time.

Are you between your eyes? In a spatial sense you are, but though embodied, you may well feel apart from your body. Your body is a physical bracket where between your right and your left you find yourself in residence. My body itself dangles somewhere between my innermost inside (my private, ongoing, upwelling fount of "me") and my not-me outside. My mind can identify with the body, making it "me," or disidentify, making the body "it." Mind, it seems, can turn its attention to various points of suspension, the brackets wherein mind minds itself. It all depends on where you place the brackets. I always find myself in some frame of mind.

But sometimes, it seems, it's more a matter that I've been framed.

The temporal brackets of this body's birth and death are, despite any wishes to the contrary, givens. I, in my waking frame of mind, cannot see before that birth, nor after that death. I am caught, ineluctably it seems, by the clock. Ineluctably, hickory, dickory, dock:* no escape.

The Tibetans claim otherwise. Birth to death is one between; death to birth another. Death is no terminus, no obliterating annihilation. Instead, the further mysterious *bardo* that spans death to rebirth closes an entrapping circle of time. Not just caught by the clock in this life, it's for life after suffering life for æons of rebirth—except, they say, there is an escape hatch. Between death and rebirth occur not one, but three *bardos.* ([It all depends on where you place the brackets.]) First is the fleeting death-point itself, so subtle that only a highly practiced consciousness can even notice it. The death-point is the escape hatch, the door to enlightenment that allows understanding beyond duality, time and space. Mostly, consciousness re-arouses only in the second between-state of the reality-between. There experience of benign and progressively more fierce deities offers further opportunity for enlightenment, unless fearful self-clinging predominates. That being the case, one flees to the third, the existence-between, which culminates at the flash-point moment of conception when the blue drop of one's mutating spiritual essence merges simultaneously with the white drop of the father's semen and the red drop of the mother's ovum. Another birth.

Harumph, you may react, to so much ungrounded metaphysical speculation. The Tibetans ground it, however, in the remaining three of the six customary *bardo* realms: the quotidian waking consciousness that frames our days from birth to death; the dreaming consciousness that opens the elsewhere of our nights; and the meditative consciousness that can carry the mind from duality to enlightenment.

Let's begin with the break of day. You find yourself as a self with the world and others around you. You need sustenance, shelter, the protection of your body. You have things to do, people to meet, alliances, arrangements, endeavors. As much as you can, you figure things out, arrange them to suit yourself and your culture. You put in a good day, let's hope, and go to sleep expecting another.

Then at night dreams come. Most you may forget when once you wake again; some you remember. During the dreaming it feels usually that the dream is real: you feel the impingement of your predicaments, your fears and hopes in reaction, your efforts to take action. Sometimes you are you while dreaming, though perhaps in a younger body, or further transformed. Sometimes you may watch yourself while dreaming, as if you are elsewhere, or in two places at once. Strange, dreams are, sometimes while dreaming, more often upon waking, when, without attention, dreams clear like the morning mist.

That can be all. Sleep, wake, sleep, wake until the sleeper wakes no more. Without attention, without the particular turnings of attention developed and practiced through meditative consciousness, forgotten dreams and too-soon forgotten days seem likely all there is: unawakened mind.

Meditation entails concentration and contemplation.* Concentration begins with holding one thing in mind—perhaps the breath—and ends, perhaps, with holding in mind holding itself, a contemplative beholding. Held, the frame of mind finds interstices, overlooked chinks in the seeming cohesiveness of what is, chinks through which to peer. One thing in mind could be a visualization, ever more complex until experienced as a world and reality of its own. The meditator, all the while aware of sitting in meditation in a particular place at a particular time, is also elsewhere: in the breath perhaps, or in the dream. Two places at once. Two places as one. (No place at all?)

The mind in meditation is a vehicle, they say—our funicular again—that can traverse the betweens. Try it, the Tibetans say, make mind your vehicle, go between. Find out for yourself. It just takes practice. Find your own groundedness, though it may be that the grounds for groundedness are shifting beneath your feet like a crumbling scree. (It [all] depends on where you place the brackets.)

Meditative consciousness, however, is not exclusively an arcane achievement of the disciplined adept. Aspects of it are common in reverie and daydreams and fantasy, and perhaps in prayer, and certainly in the psychoanalytic situation of saying what comes to mind. It involves a loosening of association, a kind of mental drifting, yet a determined openness to observe how one proliferative association leads to another in the stream of consciousness, how one thought or feeling gives way to the next. It entails a paradoxical willingness not to will, like Freud's "evenly hovering attention." One lets go in one way, while hanging on in another. Forgoing expectation and explanation permits a wandering into the unknown.

One explorer of the between was an early devoté of Freud, a young German, Herbert Silberer.* In 1909 after a splendid lunch he lay drowsily on his couch trying to compare Kant's and Schopenhauer's conceptualizations of time (an endeavor guaranteed to knock many a man out almost instantaneously). He could sketch out Kant's main points, turn adumbratively to the Schopenhauer, then turn back to find his recollection of Kant a complete blank. Thereupon came a dream-like image: he is asking a morose secretary for information; the man at first ignores him, then gives him a spurning glance. *Aha,* realizes Silberer, here is a method to traverse between the concerns of waking thought and the symbols of dreams! By sustaining his effort to think even while drifting towards sleep, he can witness how the blank puzzlement of his waking thought translates into the information-witholding secretary of his dream.

His explorations continue. At a later time he drowsily reflects that the purpose of his metaphysical studies is to work through layers of consciousness in search of the very springboard of existence. A hypnagogic reverie intervenes: he runs a long knife under a layer cake as though to lift a well-cut slice out of it. He suspends himself between the image and waking thought to consider: the layers are kinds of consciousness; the cutting is his working through; and carefully sliding the knife under the cake exposes the foundational springboard of existence.

Silberer sought his foundational springboard of existence in vain. Like Freud, he tended to reduce the dream to a symbolic representation of waking life. Waking consciousness was primary, and dream imagery important only insofar as it reflected waking concerns. Overlooked is the knife itself, that dangling vehicle of incisive attention, the mind that can be (even if by flickering oscillation) in two places at once, both awake and across the threshold of sleep. What Silberer sought, the Buddha is said to have found.

The mind that hangs onto waking remembrance while letting go of the waking world to enter the reality of the dream world, that is the mind of lucid dreaming. While dreaming, you know you dream. And knowing you dream while dreaming also gives you some power to change the dream. The dream doesn't just happen to you; you happen to it. For the Tibetans,* developing such a state of mind is another aspect of meditative practice, a dream yoga.

Yet some few people are spontaneous lucid dreamers. One Dutchman* describes his excitement at realizing lucidity for the first time: in the dream he runs up to a taxi driver shouting, "I'm dreaming. This is all a dream. You are part of my dream!" and the taxi driver, understandably since he has been confronted by a lunatic, rolls up the window and speeds away. The "I" who appears in the dream is not synonymous with the "I" who is dreaming; the "I" who knows both sways somewhere between. The dangling "I" is open, being both "I's" and neither, like a word repeated after itself so often that it starts to become a strange sound, divorced from meaning. (Try it. Say "I" fifty times.)

What accompanies, nay, constitutes a frame of mind, be it waking or dreaming, is an enframing reality. The insomniac and the dreamer both move in realms of the real. Reality for the one comprises tousled sheets and the unrelenting concerns of the day; for the other, who knows? The dream is real in its own terms, in its own spewing stream of consciousness, a world unto itself. That world may seem less predictable than the waking world, until one reflects, uneasily, that even awake one never really knows what happens next. Normal dreaming enfolds the dreamer in a reality of the night, day mind forgotten. When a nightmare scares one out of one's wits, one finds oneself, witlessly, awake. New reality: day mind to the rescue. Where is the crossover, the point between?*

Awake, I remember the dream, shiver at the nightmare, but however cinematically vivid it may be, the dream has become an image in my mind, a memory, safely this side of that curious, mysterious point of the between when image becomes reality, or reality image. Or try as I might to hold in my mind (the space before me) an image of a white lotus, it is a pale simulacrum compared to the lotus that appears before me, resplendent and real. Reality, perhaps, reflects a threshold of complexity. An image is relatively flat and fixed, an unchanging representation, while the thing itself is no fixed thing, but a complex interweaving of fluctuating threads of attention. I notice the white petals, their velvety texture, the secret moonlit throne of golden pistils inside, the waxy smell, the visiting dragonfly (like my mind) hovering in the humid, honey air at the surface of the pond. And when there is too much to notice piece by piece, when the complex connections interweave unconsciously, my consciousness finds itself facing a reality. Everything is just there. I find everything automatically sprung up before me, and like me, given. The lotus bobs on ripples that surprise me, coming, as they do, out of nowhere, and I am—where? In a dream? Or fresh off the bus, a languid tourist at the Vale of Kashmir in the summer of 1972? (It all depends [on where you place the brackets].) I am in some enfolding reality, for sure, though I may not be sure as to how or when or what. Or I may be too sure, certain that my reality is the firm ground subtending all that really is. Thank you very much, but we'll have no new realities today, please, and don't call again tomorrow.

Lucid dreaming, then, reflects a human capacity to become experientially enmeshed in the complexity of a reality, while at the same time to transcend that reality. The capacity may serve merely to bring back memorabilia, like snapshots from the dreamworld that can gather dust on the familiar mantle of my waking day. Or the capacity may go further. In view of that turnabout point between realities, like the subtle point between inhalation and exhalation when neither in nor out applies, lucidity may go both ways. The dusty mantle might start to shimmer. Lucid dreaming is one crossover. Cross back, and its counterpart is lucid waking.

Lucidity, then, is not an aspect of waking consciousness exported to the dream-state. Nor is it an aspect of dreaming consciousness leached into waking reality. Lucidity has less to do with Silberer's layer cake of consciousness than with his springboard of existence. While awake or dreaming or in some other frame of mind, lucidity becomes an awareness of the relative betweenness of experienced reality. Lucidity finds, and transcends, the frame. Lucid waking becomes another metaphor for enlightenment. Reality is real, all right, but not the whole picture. Any one reality seems to account for everything, but does so in its own self-limiting and self-defining terms.* Some tincture of lucidity can begin to bend those terms, serving not so much to undo a given reality as to place it in a wider context. Just as the dream (if only symbolically) recasts what is going on in waking life, so is waking life tinged by the dream. (I remember baffled shock, once, upon crossing paths with another boy; I remembered thereupon his demise in a dream the night before.) The terms of waking life—what one thinks of as real—are no longer so fixedly unidimensional.

What are the terms of waking life? The Tibetans posit six realms of rebirth, that is, six states of being* one can find oneself in depending on the cumulative actions of past lives. Human being is one, and the most fortunate, since it allows the possibility of reflective release into the lucidity of Buddhahood. Animal being, by contrast, is more reactively confined to the struggle to eat or be eaten, to live, mate, and die by instinct. The remaining realms appear on the surface to be at a supernatural remove. The realm of the "hungry ghosts" is a place where beings dwell perpetually unsated, hollow bellies aching beneath throats too long and thin ever to provide for their fervid desires. Hell is the realm of fear, where all imaginable tortures plague the screaming sufferers. In another realm the "jealous gods" forever battle one another to secure the spoils and power that never forestall counterattack. Is the remaining realm, the realm of the gods, not better? There they melt in æsthetic, orgasmic bliss, exquisitely sated in pleasures. Yet their heaven, too, is a hell, because they are distracted by distractions that must someday end, and they ignore the sufferings of others.

Dismissing these realms as supernatural fantasies is one thing; recognizing them as incarcerating frames of mind is quite another.

Rebirth need not be interpreted literally as one lifetime after the next; rebirth occurs minute by minute. Here I am, for a minute. I do my best to keep myself the same, to perpetuate the familiar, allowing, of course, for some customary measure of novelty. I attend to what I usually attend to, so reminding myself that I am who I am. I can live largely by habit, bathing and dressing without a thought, what thought I do remember concerned with my usual preoccupations. My memory extends beyond the minute, of course, for by the accumulation of minutes expressing their patterns of interests, patterns of concerns, habits, proclivities, turnings of attention here and not there, by the force of habit I become who I am. The accumulation of what I have done and thought about, of whom I have known and whom allowed to matter, coalesces into a worldview, the ongoing frame of mind that is my character. My character is myself.

If my characteristic frame of mind is like an animal's you may recognize me as a brute, or a thug, or perhaps a bovine plodder. It may be I eat smelly fried chicken on the subway and drop the bones on the floor. I don't care. I don't want to know. If I am a hungry ghost, forget mere fried chicken. See me as a drug addict perpetually scrambling for my next fix. If hellish fear is my characteristic preoccupation, expect cowering withdrawal from life, or paranoid vigilance, or worse, sadistic inflictions to prove to you that hell is the way the world is. If I am a jealous god, watch out. You have, I want, I take—including your peace of mind. If I am a privileged purveyor of *noblesse oblige,* beware my blandishments, my invitations to Elysian estates where we wake in the morning and our lives have passed, the champagne drunk, the party too soon over. We neglect to notice until too late the uninvited guests of sickness, aging, and death, who embrace us unprepared.

These frames of mind are caricatures, but allowing for greater nuance and variability, each can describe a character, someone like you or me. One's character is one's habitual presentation of self, variable by mood and circumstance, yet unitary in self-recognition. The Buddha saw self as a dependent phenomenon, arising from attention to the interplay of the physical senses and consciousness. Just so,

Freud saw self as buoyed on its possibilities of association—on what attention could find to turn to. The neurotic self, accordingly, suffered from unfree associations, blocked by fear or aversion from turning attention to forbidden desires. The work of psychoanalysis is to free associations. The work of Buddhism is to free associations beyond what Freud ever dreamt.

Whenever I find myself, I find myself in some frame of mind. (It all depends on [where you place the] brackets.) I contextualize the ongoing present by marking out some recognizability in place and time. Automatically, like a good journalist, I establish coördinates as to who, what, where, when, and how it's all happening. Globally, I establish my worldview. If, humanly, I am able to notice that I am doing so, then I recognize my human choice. The choice is either to assimilate everything to fit my worldview, or to accomodate my worldview to the wider unseen. I have a choice. I might choose psychoanalysis to see through some constraints of character. I might choose Buddhism to see through other habituated ways of construing reality—to know form, in fact, as emptiness.

If my experience of self is the upshot of a fluctuating associational matrix, my self is like a swarm of bees.* No particular bee directs the swarm. Indeed, the swarm seems to move with a will of its own. The swarm (though empty) is a buzzing, whirring cloud, finding its own way across some flowery meadow in our image-making minds. We can choose to attend to it in our mind's eye. We have this choice.

We are free, by degrees, to turn attention where we will. Some choices are deeply ingrained, others less so. Yet we still have some measure of choice as to what to pay attention to. Our choices, understood as choices, become hugely important, because choices have consequences. Choices construe realities, open and close possibilities, both for oneself and for everyone else. Choice entails responsibility. The choice comes between us, facing you and me with what we are to do with one another.

I can choose to assimilate you. (Resistance is futile.) I can choose to treat you as someone who is the same as others I have known. Indeed, your being "other" to me is one way you are knowable, the same as all those others. My knowing constricts, pegs, identifies you. You become an object, known to me.

Or I can choose to accommodate to you, recognizing your difference, your unknowability. I cannot become, but only imagine your "I." You persist in being different, more than I imagine. In you I encounter Thou. Between us lie mysteries, myriad opening possibilities. You see me in ways I cannot see myself. You show me who I am, and I you, and each form, each manifestation of being, is partially true for a while, while fading mysteriously away to give way to new forms of self, forms formed then fading into remembered ghosts of the way we were while still, even now, we find ourselves forming, being human, forming out of the upwelling flow of experience that just comes all by itself fully formed out of nowhere. We find ourselves born in a world we did not make, being in and of that world, come out of nowhere, just here like that (splat!), and changing by the moment, fading into memory, memory soon to be forgotten, me and you and all our yesterdays nowhere once again.

Not no-where, now-here, I need you. You hold me in mind. We have each in the other a resting place.

My choice is not simply to assimilate or to accommodate, of course. I must do both. I must keep some things constant, such as what is food and where to find it, how not to fall off cliffs, how not to be pierced by sharp objects. Surely I know a few things. After all, I wasn't born yesterday (or was I?). Problems arise when I get too certain, and in particular, when I get too certain about you. When I forget that my certainties are assumptions, I treat you as if you were just the same as ever, my known quantity with knowable variations, your difference, your mystery, neglected.

Freud calls it "transference": my proclivity to jam your being into templates from my past. I had better be on guard—you are likely trying to do the same thing to me. I had really better be on guard, says the Buddha: Unless I pay attention, I am likely trying to do the same thing to myself.

I try to keep permanent what is impermanent. I cling, perhaps, to my glorious "me" festooned with medals and merit badges, or alternatively, to my despised "me," fault-ridden and shameful. Either way, I have at least some comfort (so I imagine) in knowing who I am. I retreat from the fear of not knowing, of finding difference rather than sameness, of finding formlessness rather than form. I retreat from the vast spaciousness of unknown possibility. The challenge is to let it be, to allow experience to flow, to let be "me" so that unfettered I open to you.

> Ah, love, let us be true
> To one another! for the world, which seems
> To lie before us like a land of dreams,
> So various, so beautiful, so new,
> Hath really neither joy, nor love, nor light,
> Nor certitude, nor peace, nor help for pain,
> And we are here as on a darkling plain
> Swept with confused alarms of struggle and flight,
> Where ignorant armies clash by night.*

The joy and the love and the light in the eyes are not out there in the world; they are between us, findable in each other, in how we allow mattering to grow between us. Ignorance obscures with suffering. We cannot know each other fully. We need to know each other better and well.

We bring to each other the possibility of affiliation.* To affiliate, in its Latin derivation, is to string a special kind of connection between us: ad, "to," and filius, "son": to adopt as a son. I choose you, or you choose me, in a way that renders our separateness incidental to the way we are volitionally joined, joined by a choice. You are of me, I of you. Everyone I have known who matters to me is an affiliation. I carry with me what it was like to be with them, whether positive, with admiration or acceptance or fondness, or negative, with repulsion or fear or disdain, on my part or theirs. Everyone other than I shows me something of how I can be. I can be someone to love, or someone to hate. My affiliations remind me of who it is I do and do not want to be. Choosing hate pits me against you, the darkling way of those "jealous gods."

Choosing love, the positive affiliation, makes caring for one another paramount. Of course, we do both in every relationship.

We choose, or discover ourselves to have chosen, both love and hate. Only when what happens to a fortified "me" assumes a less central importance does the affiliative interpenetration of you and me stand out. I am for you, you for me.* I do unto you, as unto myself. We shape each other through what we notice and how we act. We bring to each other our tangled associations of experience, including what associations each of us prompts in the other. By what we choose to express in words and actions we shape our affiliation. When we affiliate with kindness and compassion, becoming fathers and mothers to one another, we adopt one another as oneself. To adopt one another is to find in each other what we have most importantly in common—not just some bond of patrilineal blood, but moreso, the bond of our human nature, so variegated, so much the same, yet unique in each of us. Between you and me, suspending you and me over the gulf of our separateness and mysterious difference, pendulous in the space between us, we sway alike in our shared, impermanent, spangled being.

BABIES

WHAT THEY SAY

"Sometimes I can't believe how fast it's all happened."

"Are you worried?"

"It's more like I think I should be worried, but then I'm not. When I think about being with her, I just grin. It feels so right, this melting feeling. I do love her. I've fallen in love."

"You reminded me you've fallen in love before."

"I am wary about getting burnt again. Or part of me thinks I should be wary, but mostly, I mean look what's happened. This is new, not like before. We've just

had our five-month anniversary and we realized we've spent almost every night together the last four months. From the beginning it was just like falling into step together, like a natural fit between us. Which is all the more surprising when you think how different our backgrounds are, me the city boy and her raised on a ranch in Montana where there are more cows than people. And her the college drop-out and me the diligent grad student—at least I was, till I dropped out after Karen. We both dropped out. We're so much alike: what we think is funny, the way we like to tool around the city together, to cook together, just to hang out and talk. Meeting her and being with her is this immense good fortune, especially because she loves me, too."

"You are a lucky man."

WHAT THEY MAY THINK
WHILE THEY SAY
WHAT THEY SAY

As he lay on the couch he noticed the dampness in his armpits and as he rolled his shoulders to place his hands behind his head the comfortable thought rolled along that he needn't out of embarrassment hide his sweat from his analyst. His gaze drifted across the ceiling, then without reading scanned the spines of the books on the floor-to-ceiling shelves covering the wall just away from his white-socked feet. He wiggled his toes. His gaze rested on his feet while he rested from the rush to get here on time. His smile showed he was thinking of her again, of the affectionate kiss she had placed on his lips as her good-bye, of the grocery shopping he knew she was doing now, and of the meal they would later eat together. Their shared thought was that because of her roommate moving out she might leave her place and move in with him. Unthought in words, the thought of living together they would taste and talk of over dinner, already knowing each other's nervousness and anticipation and hesitancy and desire. Desire met desire. She was so close where for so long so recently there had been no one. He marveled aloud, "Sometimes I can't believe how fast it's all happened."

"Are you worried?" the analyst wondered, made alert by the sound of his own voice. He had been sleepy, somewhat sleepy. He had suppressed a yawn, lying back in his chair, feet up on the footstool, left and right fingers and thumbs

touching their mates to form an arbor over his belly, whence he had glanced over his right elbow at the other settling into the couch, past the other's feet to a book on the shelf as if supported by the other's toes, the book Irrational Despair* about which the other had once teased "How can you read these kinds of books? Shouldn't 'rational despair' be enough already?" and they had laughed together. Then lingering on despair when the other spoke he wondered about worry.

Worried? "It's more like I think I should be worried, but then I'm not." He felt his smile pressing his lips. "When I think about being with her, I just grin. It feels so right, this melting feeling." From his armpits across his chest down his arms he remembered the feel of embracing her. His loins stirred. In mind were her smile, her sparkling eyes. "I do love her. I've fallen in love."

"You reminded me you've fallen in love before." What a worrywort I am. I'm fiddling with my wedding ring, hmm. My worries? His thoughts looped to his wife, then back to the couch, to the wiggler of the white-socked toes. Here's hope. He was so devastated when he first came to see me. Can he love differently now?

"I am wary about getting burnt again." His brow creased with thoughts of Karen, those endless evenings when she'd insist they sit face-to-face to "discuss our relationship." She was always too serious, even from the start. Grace laughs. Bicycling in the dark up the riverpath* it was like we were flying. "Or part of me thinks I should be wary, but mostly, I mean look what's happened." It happens fast. We fly. "This is new, not like before. We've just had our five-month anniversary and we realized we've spent almost every night together the last four months." It doesn't make any sense that she not move in. "From the beginning it was just like falling into step together, like a natural fit between us." Amazing. His mind reminded, he saw the two of them camped out in bed, touching, talking, telling the stories of how they came through life to be there then where they were so glad to be. "Which is all the more surprising when you think how different our backgrounds are, me the city boy and her raised on a ranch in Montana where there are more cows than people." She knows how to ride a horse. She could teach me. "And her the college drop-out and me the diligent grad student—at least I was, till I dropped out." Good-bye Karen, good-bye grad school, good-bye to Me as Professor of American History, smarty-pants performer. Grace could have finished. She's not dumb. She's as smart as I am. "We both dropped out. We're so much alike:

what we think is funny,"—*the sound of her laugh*— *"the way we like to tool around the city together,"*—*we fly up the river*— *"to cook together,"*—*tonight "just to hang out and talk"*—*tonight and tomorrow and tomorrow. "Meeting her and being with her is this immense good fortune, especially because she loves me, too." In mind is the light of her eyes.*

"You are a lucky man." He is. He's open. He'll work it out. I hope. I'm smiling. Diligent grad student? He hasn't referred to himself as a student in a very long time.

MORE OF
WHAT THEY SAY
WHILE THEY THINK
THOUGHTS UNVOICED

"Thank you. You're glad for me, aren't you?"

"Yes, I am."

"So . . . We're actually thinking of moving in together."

"Tell me more."

"Her roommate is going to move out at the end of the month when their lease expires, so rather than find a new roommate, we figured since she's over all the time already, and I've got more space, why not just do it?"

"This arrangement is still tentative? Why not do it?"

"There's really no reason not to . . . Still, it's a leap of faith. I mean, for me, moving in with Karen was the deathblow to our—our 'relationship.' That's what she always called it, especially at the end when she always wanted to sit down and 'discuss our relationship.'"

"I remember."

"At that point, the way I see it now, it was like sitting down to dissect a corpse. Two years of dating, two months of living together, and then her reasoned brief 'Better For Both Of Us' if I moved out. She was such a lawyer, night and day. Ironically, though—even though I wanted us to stay together so much—she was right. Now I can see it. I'd become like her lapdog, I'm still ashamed to say."

"And with Grace?"

"I don't have that same feeling that I need to please her, to stay on her good side so that she'll put up with me. In hindsight, it was so awful my doing that

with Karen. Grace and I don't do that. I don't have to perform. I don't have to
hide anything. Neither does she. It's like we can let go with one another. Oh."

"Eh?"

"Well, I, uh, letting go, just remembered this lovemaking experience? You
know how it's been really intense and how I love her coming so easily?"

"You've said, yes."

"Well, today we woke up around noon—I'd spent part of the night with her
at the bakery again. Watching her work so comfortably with all that machin-
ery to turn out these perfect croissants, I love it."

"It's quite a process, from what you've said."

"Well, anyway. We woke up and did it, made love, I mean, only afterwards
I just sort of let go and rested inside her. We lay for a long time like that. It
was incredibly satisfying. I lifted my head back to look at her and she was smiling away at me—like I was smiling away at her, I guess. Then she shifted her
pelvis a little, sort of nuzzling me, and with these ever so slight pushes and
pulls we felt me get hard inside her again. This is hard to describe. Anyway, it
was like we didn't have to do anything, just let go. It was incredibly plea-
sureable for a really long time, and I couldn't tell where I stopped and she
started. I know it's a cliché, but it's true, the way it felt. She came with me,
like she was drinking me in. And then she was crying, which made me start to
cry, too. I asked if she was all right and she said she was happy, so very happy
to be with me. I felt so happy with her. I feel so happy. I'm tearing up just
telling you about it."

"You're open."

"You bet. I've never felt this way. Or so much this way. But you know, it's also
scary. I mean, orgasms out of the blue, how can I tell what'll happen next? And
I know I love her, but at some level I can hardly believe she loves me back. But
she does! What a gift! I maybe feel more alive than I ever have."

"What is the level that can hardly believe she loves you?"

"Let's see. Some part of me that feels crappy and rejectable."

"Any associations?"

"I've felt crappy and rejectable for most of the time you've known me. You
could say that's what brought me to analysis."

"Who is it who came to analysis? The 'rejected one'?"

"Yeah, sure. And also the 'worthless son' and the 'mama's boy' and the 'lapdog' and the 'performing professor' who can talk up such a good show. And let's not forget the 'solitary insomniac.' That might make him feel rejected."

"What happened to him? You haven't talked about insomnia for awhile. Are you neglecting the 'solitary insomniac'?"

"Ha! He's still around, but he's too tired to wake up because he's exhausted from all this sex."

"An excellent solution to his problem."

"It's funny, talking about those aspects of me. We've talked about all of them so much. But they start to seem like a gallery of strangers. It's scary to let them go, but also freeing. I'm free of their hang-ups, except that they can still show up."

"And be sent away. Sounds like part of being free is being free not to recognize yourself, not to get stuck in one of your guises."

"That's true. Only this new 'loved-by-Grace' doesn't feel like a guise. It feels like a blessing, like a call to live."

"Congratulations."

"Speaking of which, as I said 'a call to live' I flashed back to a dream I had a couple of nights ago, which now seems pretty obvious."

"Let's hear it."

"The perspective is funny, like I'm in two places at once. Mostly it's like I'm watching the whole thing like a movie, where I'm looking down on myself frozen in the ice of a river. But I can also see up through the ice."

"Frozen in the ice?"

"There's a river that's iced over, see, clear ice with the water running underneath. And I'm frozen in the ice. I'm not dead. I just can't move. But I can see through the ice to the riverbank where there are trees and someone comes out from the trees with ice skates on and starts skating in circles and loop-de-loops all around me. Through the ice I can hear the zinging sound that the skate blades make. The ice on top of me melts so I can sit up. So I sit up but I can't really make out who this skater is. I have the thought that I can skate, too. Even though I don't have skates I can skate in my shoes, so I go looping around, too, me and this skater having a really good time. That's when I woke up. I sort of played the dream back for myself so I'd remember it, then I fell asleep, and here it is again."

"You said it was obvious?"

"Well, obvious like here I was talking about Grace being a call to live and the dream pops into mind so it's like she's been the skater who's thawed me out."

"You've mentioned a 'melting feeling' a few times."

"I guess I have."

"It's curious the skater stays vague within the dream. Any associations?"

"Well, let's see. Remember when they taught me how to skate in boarding school my first winter there? That's when I did skate up the river into the woods. It was only that one year when the river froze well before snow came. Snow would cover the ice so that you couldn't skate on it. But that one year you could skate deep into the woods. And it really did zing, the sound of the skates. I loved it. I'd go way upriver."

"Alone?"

"Alone? Yes. I mean everyone else would want to stay near school and play hockey. So I'd go alone, which I preferred anyway . . . You mean, what if I'd fallen through the ice and no one had been there to rescue me? Actually, I don't suppose a rescue would have been particularly likely anyway. Besides, you could look at the ice and see where it was getting thinner, at least mostly. And the sound would change, too."

"Sounds like you knew about thin ice. Or hoped you knew. I was thinking how your mother had just died and you felt disposed of by your father. You weren't sure of your ground yet at school, not yet the honors student. You were in transition. Like the skater in your dream, you were vague to yourself."

"That's true. But also, when I got way upriver? I didn't have to define myself, or I was just me and I could forget about it, just be myself by myself and zing along."

"Maybe that's the frozen you, happy to dream alone in ice."

"I wouldn't say I was happy in the ice. I was just there. But there is something about being away from the world."

"You said the dream had two perspectives? Who's the one who was watching the whole dream like a movie?"

"That's interesting: the watcher of the world."

"The one who can see the bigger picture. Hmm. The one who lets other people in, from out of the woods?"

"That's true. I knew that skater was coming out of the woods before I saw him, from under the ice, I mean."

"Him?"

"I did say 'him' just now, didn't I? In the dream it wasn't clear. Could've been Grace, I thought."

"Maybe 'him' is also you."

"That's always true, isn't it? I mean, as you always say, it is my dream."

"Maybe 'him' is me?"

"You mean the whole dream is about analysis? That does sort of fit. Like the skater, you are vague to me in a lot of ways. And you do go in for loop-de-loops, past, present and future. And, it occurs to me, here is where I lie down on the couch and then sit up at the end of the session, like sitting up in the dream. Could be about analysis. Could be."

"So the skater could be Grace, could be you, could be me."

"All of the above. And more."

"I guess we're both watchers, too. How did you put it, 'watcher of the world'? We watch together."

"Yeah. I suppose that is what we do in here, with ourselves as part of the world, only you watch me more than I watch you what with your peculiar seating arrangement."

"I see that's our time."

"Okay. I'm thawed."

WHAT THE ANALYST
UNKNOWN TO HIMSELF
MAY DREAM IN LIKELIHOOD
ABOUT HER OF WHOM THEY SPEAK
WHILE THEY SAY
WHAT THEY SAY

One thing Grace liked about her job was its timelessness. She always removed her watch when she arrived at work, punctually at 9:00 P.M. She left her bicycle on the wide landing at the head of the basement stairs, descended to the female employees' locker room, and changed from her street clothes to her baking clothes: flannel-lined blue jeans, a heavy shirt, and her fisherman's sweater, frayed at the elbows. She wore heavy socks with her baking shoes: wooden-soled clogs white with flour. As she left the locker room she took from a laundered pile a long white apron and cloth cap.

She might stop and chat with Gerard, the pastry chef, or Maureen, busy at bread. But soon she would make her way to her own alcove in the basement bakery. Walls, floors, and ceilings were white tile, lit flourescently white with no windows permitting the intrusion of the outside world. No matter what the weather outside, her alcove was fifty-five degrees, needle steady on its industrial thermostat.

The alcove was like a dead-end corridor doglegging away from the pastry counters in such a way that Grace worked out of sight of anyone else. Against the butt-end of the alcove was the sheeter: an eight-foot-long reciprocating conveyer belt above which was mounted a vertically adjustable stainless steel rolling pin with safety bumpers on either side so that human arms would not go the way of flattened dough. To the left of the sheeter was a stainless steel door with a heavy refrigerator latch. This led not to a refrigerator, but to the proofing room, where rolling racks of coddled dough were left to rise and swell at precisely eighty degrees Fahrenheit and eighty per cent relative humidity.

Grace's timeless time ended when she rolled her racks of trays of croissants into that room. After a gestating time Luis would roll the racks into the walk-in oven, but Grace would be gone.

Her timeless time began* as she weighed out on her balance-beam scale ten kilograms of flour, two hundred grams of salt, fourteen hundred grams of granulated sugar, three hundred-fifty grams of French yeast, and half a kilo of sweet butter. She fitted the dough hook attachment to the floor-mounted Hobart mixer that stood as tall as she herself, then combined her ingredients with ten eggs in its slowly rotating knee-high stainless steel bowl. Then, all at once, she added three liters of ice water. As the dough began to clump she added a bit more water, and a bit more—perhaps a liter and a half—until it looked right to her and she added two hundred grams of salt, pouring it against the rotor in a fine stream. Adjusting a large spoked knob, she increased the machine's speed and let it run several minutes while the dough flowed hypnotically over the rotor. When the dough ball was well formed she stopped the Hobart, removed the rotor, and carried the heavy mixing bowl to her marble counter. She covered it with a towel, to rest and to rise.

Meanwhile she set up her rolling racks with parchment-lined sheet pans, like empty high-rise apartment buildings awaiting their residents. She took ten five-hundred–gram blocks of butter, and pounded each with a wooden mallet *into a flat square. She peeked under the towel, then flung it away with satisfaction. Dumped from the bowl onto her floured marble counter, the doughball quivered. Baring her arms by pushing up the sleeves of her sweater, she gathered the ball warm against her aproned belly and then punched and folded and caressed it by hand and then cut it, with practiced accuracy, into ten equal pieces. With the heels of her hands she pressed each piece flat against the counter into a shape like a fourleaved clover, into the center of which she placed a square of the butter before folding the clover leaves over to seal the butter inside. Next she carried each envelope to the sheeter, where back and forth under the huge roller she flattened and folded and flattened and folded twice more to a thickness of three-eighths of an inch her buttered dough.*

Grace cut each of the ten long narrow rectangles so formed into forty-eight triangles, by hand rolled up each triangle into a croissant, placed each croissant among three rows of four croissants each on each of the papered sheet pans, ten pans to a rack but not to the rack before she brushed each croissant with a wash of slightly beaten egg. Twelve croissants to a pan, ten pans to a rolling rack, four racks for four hundred and eighty croissants, with exactitude. She did this each timeless time, alone in her white-tiled, temperature-controlled basement alcove. Sometimes she would hum to herself, sometimes smile at her passing thoughts, and sometimes as she finally rolled rack upon rack of croissants to the proofing room, she would say fondly under her breath, "My babies. My babies."

5.

ATTACHMENTS

One conclusion was forced upon my mind at that time, and my impression
of its truth has ever since remained unshaken. It is that our normal
waking consciousness, rational consciousness as we call it, is but one
special type of consciousness, whilst all about it, parted from it by the
flimsiest of screens, there lie potential forms of consciousness entirely
different ... No account of the universe in its totality can be final
which leaves these other forms of consciousness quite disregarded.
—WILLIAM JAMES*

FRAMES OF MIND

A HUNDRED YEARS AGO William James saw rational consciousness,
so esteemed by Enlightenment thinking and the scientific method,
as a potential trap. The trap is to assume so great an attachment to
rationalism that its truths alone rule reality. Its truths *are* pertinent.
I know not to touch a hot stove. I benefit from technological progress. I share with you our common sense about whys and wherefores, about what is sane and what crazy. Yet its truths falter when I
ask why bad things happen to good people, or why there is something rather than nothing, or why I. Such questions can be dismissed
as irrational, or answered (after a leap of faith) within a mythic or
religious framework that provides rational explanations (because
God wills it so). God explains the unknowable, playing a role something like zero among the rational numbers: by having a place for
that nothing made into something, that absence indicated by an
empty circle (like a Zen circle?), the whole rational interplay of
arithmetic works. Algorithms predict with certainty. Measured

recipes make croissants. God is in heaven, and mankind on earth cosseted by a rationale for living.

It is little wonder such a worldview invites attachment. Even its polar alternative, atheism, proffers an attachment to a rational explanation of the godless way things are. To detach from rationalism would seem (rationally) to risk insanity, or death. To recognize frames of mind, including quotidian consciousness, as formations dependent on the "flimsiest of screens" risks experiencing mind unframed.

The Buddha (so we are told) took that risk, finding a way to live rationally in the world, and simultaneously, to be otherwise, beyond, frameless. The way of psychoanalysis, I maintain, by lifting a corner of one flimsy screen that conceals the unconscious, opens consciousness to an ongoing process of reframing. Both ways flirt with the dissolving of attachments to particular frames of mind, thereby allowing some greater experience of inconceivable (since a concept is a frame) framelessness.

This chapter begins with a brief meditation on attachment. The meditation leads to a consideration of Buddhist attachment, and in particular to a consideration of nonattachment in the story of the life of the Buddha, and, speculatively, to where the Buddha's choices left his son, Rahula. Rahula's plight is ours from the psychoanalytic perspective on attachment next discussed. Both the Buddhist and the psychoanalytic perspectives lead to ethical conclusions as to how we are to be with one another in the world.

A Brief Meditation

Breathing.

Breathing in, breathing out, and in, and out, and . . .

Atop the breathing arises "I."

I could hold my breath, alter its cadence, depth, sound, until my attention wanders, and where my attention goes go I. Unattended, left to itself, is breathing, empty of "I."

I return. I tether my attention to the breathing, in and out, in and out. Tethered, "I" can be unattended, left to itself, emptied. Without holding, I let be breathing. Without holding breathing beholds.

Holding is a grasping. Beholding is a witnessing.

These thoughts carry me here and there; here and there I find myself, feeling familiarly this way and that, holding these thoughts as mine. Holding thoughts, I am. I think I am?* Let them go, let them pass. Let me go.

Return to breathing. The breath goes in, the breath goes out. I need do nothing.

A breath-catching thought: someday the breath will stop. No breath will let me pass. No breath will let me go.

Thought to thought to thought races along, forming "I" the thinker in thought's quick wake. I can hold to thought, pushing and shaping and polishing, or I can unhold thought, letting what comes go.

Let go the thought. Return to breathing's in and out. Let me go. Just now no need for me. Now, just breathing.

Breathing.

RAHULA'S PLIGHT

What kind of father abandons his wife and newborn son? The Buddha did. He named his son Rahula, which means "fetter." His pleasure palace spoiled by his confrontation with the inevitability of sickness, aging, and death, the Buddha, myth has it, at age twenty-nine renounced his family, riches, and princely status to wander as a homeless, mendicant yogi. Six years passed. Ascetic privations had replaced indulgence. His bones protruded. His eyes sank in their sockets like water in a deep well. Then, meditating beneath a tree, flesh mortified, death a breath away, he chose to eat.*

He had realized that attachment to deprivation, like attachment to indulgence, obscured the wisdom of a "middle way" between greed and aversion. Wisdom could counter ignorance, generosity replace greed, compassion trump aversion. He ate the milk-rice freely proffered by a local woman. His awakening had begun. Nourished, he moved to meditate under a nearby bodhi tree, vowing not to move until he beheld the truth of existence. Through the long night, the evil deity Mara tried to lure him with temptations and assault him with armies, but his equanimity remained undisturbed. At dawn, in an instant, the Buddha is enlightened. He says, not I, but "It is enlightened." He is moved to touch the earth with his fingertips. He arises to teach for the next forty years the truth he has discovered.*

Yet what of Rahula, the little boy left to grow up without a father? Legend* has it that the Buddha with a large retinue returned to the city of his birth seven years after leaving it. His wife, Yasodhara Bimba, feels abandoned anew by his not coming directly to see her. Her concerns involve what other people must think: that she was abandoned in the first place because she must have been a bad wife; that she and her son, like a widow and an illegitimate child, were persons of no merit in society; that her husband's begging for alms would demean the family in others' eyes; that she had lost her beauty and so her worth. She refuses to come when the Buddha's father sends for her. She is ready to die of humiliation. Informed of her distress, the Buddha returns to their palace. He takes his seat on the red-draped throne under a canopy bejeweled with diamonds, rubies, emeralds, flecks of gold, opals, sapphires, and amethysts.

Yasodhara's servants tell her of her husband's return. She feels hot, short of breath, fans herself with her scarf. She dresses carefully, and arranges her hair. She takes Rahula by the hand, and enters the throne room. Upon first laying eyes on the Buddha, she is angry and resentful. She collapses in rageful tears, complaining of her abandonment, her loneliness, his lack of compassion for her, for his son Rahula, whom she invites to go with her so they may die together.

Then she slowly comes forward, and respectfully bows her head down to the Buddha's feet. Undoing her long hair, with it she brushes the dust from the Buddha's feet. She tells him she is ashamed, and unlucky.

Gradually, in the face of the Buddha's teachings, Yasodhara's sorrow disappears as her spiritual realization grows. Rahula, too, comes to deep understanding, and is ordained by his father. They are not singled out. They are ones among the others in the wandering retinue of his disciples. So goes the legend.

The story demonstrates a complicated lesson in the nature of attachment: attachment and detachment are like two sides of the same coin; where there is the one, there is the other. Further, only *non*attachment provides freedom from suffering. Let me clarify.

Rahula is like a fetter in that he can chain the Buddha to a defining domesticity. Domesticity has its pleasures. The Buddha must detach himself from that attachment in order to find freedom. Pleasure abjured, ascetic deprivation substitutes. Ironically, the determined deprivation becomes in itself an attachment. Detachment from pleasure is the same as attachment to pain. Detachment from more becomes attachment to less; detachment from less becomes attachment to more. How abjure attachment? Through the nonattachment of the middle way. Pleasures and pains come and go unclung to. Mara's seductions prompt no lust, his armies no fear in the empty being of nothing to lose and nothing to gain, perfect and complete as is. When the Buddha upon enlightenment touches the ground, he marks his closeness to the earth: he is where he is.

When he returns to the city of his birth, his not rushing back to wife and son demonstrates a quality of nonattachment. Yasodhara sees this as cruel indifference, or at least lack of compassion, in particular because of her attachment to concerns about what the neighbors might think. She is attached to appearances. The Buddha sits on his former throne out of compassion for her: only by appearing in this way* can she understand he has returned, though he is not as she would have him be. Diamonds and rubies hold no allure. When, with quiet respect, she approaches the throne to dust his feet with her hair, this is no submissive abasement. She is not making herself lower than the Buddha from shame; her shame is over her self-grasping efforts to make herself higher. She dusts his feet with what had been the vanity of her hair. She shows the same humility the Buddha showed in touching the earth. She is near the ground, with the ground, of the ground, respectfully here with all else on earth.

Yet what of Rahula, the little boy left to grow up without a father? The legend has his mother do the talking. In the end, he is taken care of, as is she (as are we?), by the teaching of the Buddha. Let us imagine, however, by way of projecting our time and place onto that long-ago child, what his attachments might have been had his father never come back. What was Rahula's plight?

His very name is a ball-and-chain. Because of his name he stands out, unlike anyone else. He knows his father abandoned his mother and himself to go on a renunciatory quest. He sees her anger, resentment, and loneliness, hears her complaints of ostracism and disparagement.

He can attach himself to her version of reality. The two of them are suffering, and his father is to blame. His peculiar name is his father's curse on him, as if he himself is a hindrance to be rejected. He can hate his father for that, for the selfishness of leaving, for the pain to his mother, for the vacuum in his life.

Or Rahula might give it little thought, keep the whole thing out of mind. He could have it worse than growing up in a pleasure palace. And if his father abandoned him, in his mind he can abandon his father.

Or Rahula might idealize his father. His name could be a blessing in disguise, a reminder to renounce the confining shell of what people call him. His father's must be a heroic quest to slay the dragon of inevitable suffering. His father's leaving must show courage, strength, and determination.

The one sort of attachment is to hatred: father becomes the enemy and the other, unlike oneself. The thoughtless attachment is to ignorance, the supposition that what you don't know won't hurt you. The idealizing attachment is a kind of greed, aggrandizing oneself through connection to the aggrandized.

Rahula's plight is to find some sort of attachment, some way of defining his father and thereby himself in relation to his father, so that he can know who he is. His hope is to know *I am my father's son*. His deeper plight is that because his father is absent, he cannot know his father, and so cannot know who he is. His attachments are stopgap compromises. At base, Rahula must face not knowing. He cannot hold fixed his absent father. His plight deeper still is that even were his father present, he cannot hold fixed his father. His father is other than himself, a mystery. Just so is each of us a mystery to the other.

Ironically, when his father does come back, Rahula encounters no solution but an exaggeration of the mystery. Who is the Buddha? Not merely his father, but the Awakened One, and one awakened to what can be named but not known except in a firsthand experience ill described as knowing. Another person remains other than oneself, a mystery. And mysteriously further, one can become other to oneself.

Rahula's attachments stop the gap between himself and the other, quashing mystery, providing familiar knowability. The lesson of non-attachment opens the gap to emptiness. When expedient attachments dissolve, unknowingness fades the known. The opening of that gap seemingly threatens constancy, rational certainty, my being there with you alongside me. And yet, here we are, sprung into being, fathered and mothered, present, sharing breath for some brief time being.

Touch the earth. Rahula's plight is our own.

PSYCHOANALYTIC ATTACHMENT

We exist in curlicues of thought, filigrees of mentalization.* We warm our heads with skullcaps knit from the threads of stories.* Let me tell you what happened when. The story of my life defines me. We'll both have a protagonist to hang onto. I lie on the couch and speak.

You don't speak back. Are you listening? I'll suppose so. Where are you? You sit somewhere behind my head, a blankness behind me. You are other than I, a blankness not filled in, while I tell you so much about myself. It is for you, I am filling myself in. You speak now and then, as if in recognition. Do you like me? Am I all right? I do not feel all right. In the story of my life something is awry. Aha, you are interested. Your listening suggests the story of my life is not all filled in. I have forgotten things, yes. Memory changes the story. The story is memory. Some things I won't tell you, things that touch too hard on shame, my not being the way I want to be. Maybe I will tell you. Maybe it's safe. Some things I might tell you. Some things I won't tell myself. I must save face.

What face is there to save? You are other than I. The face you see I cannot see. The face you see is other than mine.* I can hide behind it. You'll never truly see my face. But shall I? How can I? I cannot see my face. You speak. What you say feels right. The face you see I can see through your eyes. You speak. It feels wrong. The face you see I can only see with changes I now fill in. You speak. You wrong me, but maybe not, when your wrong is right, and my right erodes, allowing wrong to right it. I lie more barefaced, unless unknowingly still to myself I lie. We speak, time and again, me on the couch, you in the chair, not looking at each other's faces except in mind.

The filling in is endless. I see myself this way, I see myself that. You add the other: I see myself in other ways than I had ever conceived. You stay with me.

I see you this way, that. Knowing little about you, I know you, more and more. Knowing much about me, regardless, you know me more and more. Who is it we know?

I don't know who you are. I know, more and more, how you are with me. I know how you can be.

However much I tell you, I don't know who I am, because your blankness can hold always more. More changes the story. Who I am, at base, is *sans* base. I am not who I think I am. I am not what I say, not any of the stories I tell. Perhaps I am how I tell them. I know, more and more, how I am with you. I find how I can be, free of the story, in blankness.

The stories spin along, *blah blah,* lilting *blah,* enticing *blah.* Blankness holds them all, with always room for more. Blankness stays, silence returns. I open my lips, my tongue shapes breath to sound, to make in you my story, in you to make myself, in blankness we are found. Silence.

You say this, I say that. I try to shape you this way and that, and you me, to confine each other to stories, until sometimes we let go the stories, to let each other be, non-attached, unstoried, present, not doing or done to, not held but beheld. When session ends, it may be, I go, non-attached. We are just how we are. Freed up, how we say what we say reveals a style, a uniqueness, a difference between us that keeps us always other to one another, yet the same in how we are.* Your otherness confronts me. I can reject, ignore, or desire you, attaching you to my own ends. Or respecting your otherness, I can seek you, and find in you, in how I am with you and how you are with me, how it is I am.

Beholding Each Other

My greatest attachment is to my life itself. No life, no me. I can grasp for life in the direst of circumstances. I can cling to my going-on-being until I drop with exhaustion into that dreamless sleep I surmise to be like death. Yet from that sleep I arise through dreams each day again to find now and here my me. I can count, it seems, on me. Embodied, altered, aging, I am propelled by desires, repelled by aversions, impelled to defend what I assume I know: me. Tyranically, I know the world is mine to use: for food, for pleasure, for a passing whim. Others are there to serve and please me. Let them do it well or beware. I dream to rule the world.

Then the world intrudes on me. In pain, I shriek in helpless rage. The world is bigger and will not obey. Others are recalcitrant, or force their rule on me. I get what I can, keeping an eye out for me in this life so brutish and short.

Then I find you. At first, we agree, if I use you, you may use me. We cover each other's backs: no arrows from behind. And then, if fortune grants us rest and time, we find each the other, too, like me. You want, you fear, you think you know, like me. Like me, you are, and so I like you. We like each other, and like still more when we are more than two. We become a tribe alike, know our likes likewise dislikes, know what we like quite well. We keep the same and oust the others. We rule. And yet it may come our tribe sees other tribes as us.

Still the world intrudes. My liking cannot keep it so. My best-laid plans teeter on the unplanned flux of change. One day I don't awake. Or you. My friend, my self, my me, good-bye.

Awake so much as we may be, we teeter at the brimming edge where time spills gone to timelessness. Dump the stuff, the possessing possessions not worth the time. Cut loose the attainments, the frippery and pride. In the end we travel light, even bodies left behind, if in the end we travel.

All we have is now, and in this now each other. Shantideva said it centuries ago: "Hands and other limbs/Are thought of as the members of a body./Shall we not consider others likewise—/Limbs and members of a living whole?"*

Must we cling in desperation? Flesh cannot cling forever to the bone. How best to use what time there is, one's granted measure of a lifetime? One's life is for the other.

A story* has it that a monk met in the forest a tiger. Fleeing for life he slipped from the edge of a cliff. Fortunately, he grabbed a bush to break his fall. The tiger paced above, growling hungrily. Below, far below, waited death in a rushing river. Unfortunately, the bush's roots began to yield. The monk noticed, before his nose, growing in a crack of the cliff, a perfect strawberry. Has he the presence of mind to eat it? Not eating it could signify the grip of fear. Yet to eat it could be mere recourse to sensual gratification, an indulgent distraction from his dilemma. Or, like a middle way, the eating of the strawberry could be an embrace of his dilemma, living and dying at once, open to impermanence. The meaning of the act depends entirely upon the monk's presence of mind.

Each of us, oblivious or not, is the monk. For each of us, with each moment, time's up. The responsibility is ours, to choose to panic, deny or distract, or to choose more fully to live. Further, each of us, oblivious or not, is the strawberry, grown a lifetime, found now interleaved in the world.

In Buddhism, a conscious recollection of generosity, patience, compassion, sustained diligence, meditation, and wisdom (the virtuous perfections or *paramitas*) informs one's actions so as to live responsibly, lessening the suffering of others and so of oneself. One's life occurs in relation to the other.

Psychoanalysis prescribes no conscious recollection of virtues. Yet in psychoanalysis, too, whatever has happened and whoever may be to blame, the discovery awaits that one is responsible for one's life now, from now, for better or for worse. There is some freedom to act, some freedom to change. One can become other than the self one seemingly had to be. How one is with the analyst, how one is with others, defines how one is. In confrontation with the other one confronts oneself.* One's life occurs in relation to the other.

The other is the analyst. The other is the guru. The other is the orphan, the widow, the stranger, the enemy and the friend, the infant and the corpse. The way of suffering is to defend one's separateness by self-centered clinging, while immuring the other in otherness. Surcease of suffering lies in recognizing the other as the same, finding otherness in oneself. The spark of recognition is a light in the eyes.

All we have is now, and in this now each other. We can close now down, replaying old realities, by habit overlooking one another, taking one another for granted. We can remain attached to what has been, or attached to our insistencies as to what must be. Or we can risk difference, dare to look in each other's eyes, there to find ourselves in the flux of spangled, shimmering, limpid being, just so, just as it is.

OUR LOVE

"She's pregnant."

"Pregnant?"

"We found out this morning, with one of those drug store test kits."

"How do you feel?"

"Just at this moment, I don't know. I mean part of me feels like an idiot. What was I thinking?"

"How do you mean?"

"Well, about birth control."

"I thought you were using condoms."

"That was true when we first got together. But it was such a drag to have anything at all between us. Her periods were like clockwork—until now—so we'd figured we were safe at the beginning and tail end of her period. And the middle? I guess sometimes we'd remember and sometimes we just wouldn't think about it."

"Just wouldn't think?"

"How's that for someone who's in analysis and should be so self-reflective and all? That's how I feel like an idiot . . . Also, I'm stunned. We both are. I mean, we've been together most of a year, and we've talked about getting married someday in the future—always in the future—only here's this pregnancy now."

"Why do you think you weren't thinking?"

"I don't know. I haven't thought."

"Give it a go. What if you'd consciously thought during lovemaking, 'We could get pregnant.'"

"But not now! I'm not ready. How about the practicalities? Like the money when she stops working? Like medical expenses? How can I afford a kid in the city?"

"I'm confused. That's what you would have consciously thought, or that's what you think now?"

"Both! How are we going to manage this?"

"Are you assuming that you'll have the baby?"

"Looks like it. Without even thinking about it! When she first came out of the bathroom, after the test, I mean, she just nodded yes, sort of looking at me tentatively. And I nodded yes, and we broke out in this big grin, each of us. Then she screamed, not scared, but with excitement. Or maybe scared. But excited, too. Which is what I feel: really really excited. Let's do it! We're going to have a baby. The scary part is how. I mean, how are we going to take care of this baby? I mean, the clock is ticking, this baby is coming along in—what is it—more or less nine months, and it's here."

"If the pregnancy proceeds well."

"You are such a worrywort. Of course, you're right. That's another thing to worry about. Plus she'll have to stop working. My job as a word-processor is not exactly lucrative. Neither of us has medical insurance. We also thought how it's a five-flight schlep from the street up to my loft, which will be a dilly with a baby. Her parents are not likely to be pleased with the out-of-wedlock aspect of things. I don't know about my father. I don't know how he'll react. Maybe the way I'm reacting, asking myself 'What am I doing?'"

"I'm struck by how little you seem to think about not having a baby now."

"You mean have an abortion and get pregnant when everything else is all tidy and in place?"

"That's one option. 'All tidy' doesn't sound like it holds much appeal."

"Grace did raise it, at first, but it just seemed like, no, that's not what we're going to do. It's not about abortion. It's about our baby, about our having a baby together which seems utterly extraordinary. How could we pass this up? When I think about its being this little combination of her and me growing alive in the world?"

"The same yet separate."

"Yeah. Part of our lives carrying on apart from us. Our love. It's funny to think of it that way: we made love. We made a love. We can love this kid and help it—him or her—grow up and go out into the world. I can love doing this together with Grace. I mean, if I let myself go, I can see her with the infant in her arms, and feel the little hand in mine learning to walk, and think of picnics in the park and first days of school. This gets sentimental really quick, doesn't it? But why not? It feels really good."

"You're letting yourself go into a dream of the future, I guess. I'm reminded of the way you described yourself in your ice dream, as a 'watcher of the world.'"

"While being in the world I'm watching. The sentimental stuff is great, but I'm not forgetting the dirty diapers. They tell me once you have a kid, the thing is, you have it. This is going to change everything."

"A change you've wanted, isn't it? Even though you've been ambivalent enough not to think about it. Or to have it occur to you in your thoughts here. Maybe underneath it all you've really wanted this baby quite awhile."

"I suppose so. For both Grace and me, too. It feels really right. We want this."

"It's also a kind of rebirth within you. What's it like to think of yourself as a father?"

"Me a father? First thought is I'm going to do a better job than my old man. Which should only require being around. I do wonder how he's going to react to this. I think I can be a good father. The thing is, I'll want to be around. I think I know what it is I was missing as a boy, and so I have a chance to become the father I wish I'd had. At least I hope so. On the other hand, you never know what's going to happen, do you?"

"Not for certain."

"So I'm faced with it: making the best of the situation I find myself in. The best thing going for me is being in love with Grace. No question. And now the baby comes along as part of that. Don't get me wrong. I'm not just *assuming this baby will come along easy as can be and grow up a wonder child. Anything could happen. You're right about the pregnancy. Hell, even this drugstore test guaranteed ninety-nine per cent accurate could be wrong—is wrong, one time in a hundred. Of course, Grace did it again and it came out positive again. And even as we speak, she's at the doctor's getting a blood test. It's really sort of simple. We want to do what we can to make everything turn out the best we know how. And we're in it together, through thick and thin."*

"So you're less scared than excited?"

"I guess so. When you get right down to it, choosing the baby means choosing to work at setting things right. I don't have time to quake and shiver and feel incompetent. I'm done with that—at least that's the way I feel right now. I'm sure I'll have relapses. But freaking out does me no favor and it's no help to Grace and this potential babe. It's time to get my act together."

"Haven't you been?"

"Yeah. And you've been helping me. But now it's showtime."

"What does that mean?"

"It means that I actually have been thinking about answers to the question 'What am I doing?' Like money. I need a real job. And let's remember I do have a Master's in history and can use it to get a job teaching in high school."

"You had thought of that when you first took the word-processing job."

"I couldn't have taught then. Let's face it, I might've had the credential, but I didn't have the courage."

"You needed more time to lick your wounds."

"And times change. There's a demand for teachers. I like kids. I can do this. If a particular school doesn't work out, I can move along. And I still love history. It's worthwhile to me. I can do this."

"Sounds good."

"And that'll give me health insurance. We'll need to get married, better sooner than later. That'll please her parents—that'll please us. I'll be 'husband' as well as 'father.' Now that sounds good. I figure we'll just get the license and have a party. Or maybe some sort of ceremony. Do you think you'd want to come?"

"To your wedding?"

"Yes."

"What are your thoughts about it?"

"You are really important to me. It's because of you that I am where I am now, I mean, that I'm even ready to get married."

"That's our work together. It takes two to tango."

"Yeah, but you really have helped me. So I'd be really pleased to have you there on such a big occasion. Would you come?"

"Let me think about it. I am happy for you. It'd be fun. But then I think again about our work together: meeting only in this room, our focus on what comes to your mind, my knowing about the people in your life only through the ways you describe them. It seems important to preserve that."

"Hmm. Maybe so. I didn't think of it that way. Besides, I suppose it could be rather awkward for you to walk around among all these people you know a lot about and they don't know you. You couldn't even introduce yourself as my analyst, could you, without breaking confidentiality? Unless I introduced you. Maybe that would be sort of strange. 'Dad, I'd like you to meet——' He would flip out. I'm assuming he doesn't care to have you know so much about him. And he's even footing most of the bill for it. But Grace, she'd be happy to meet you."

"I wish her well."

"You know, when I think about your not being there, it's not like you're not there. I mean, I imagine thinking of you at this party or whatever, as if you were there despite not being physically present. And of course I have it in mind to tell you about the party when we do meet, so it's like part of me is watching the party with you. You're there."

"Now we're both 'watchers of the world.'"

"Yeah. That's what we do from up here in this room. But at this point it's almost like the room is this permanent place in my mind, and you're always there for me. I can always come here, to this room, even if I'm not physically present."

"Eerie, isn't it?"

"Also, comforting . . . You know what?"

"What?"

"Maybe I'm done."

"How do you mean?"

"Well, I was thinking about telling you about the wedding party after the party, and at that point my being a husband, which made me think about being *able to pay my own way, including your fee, which I could actually do if I were a teacher and had health insurance instead of my dad to cover some of your bill, but then I thought how I'm not going to be in analysis forever. I'm going to be a dad myself, and the thought of being a dad doesn't jibe with being in analysis somehow. There's always more to talk about, but then thinking of myself as a dad it's like there's work to do and stuff, and I don't actually need to talk to you when I know where you are. Or is it who you are? I can always refer to you when I know that you're in this room in my head. So I don't actually need to see you. Does that make any sense?"*

"I think so. It does make sense. How does it feel?"

"Eeek! What am I doing? In one day I discover I'm a father and I plan to get married and now I'm talking about stopping analysis. Isn't this a bit much?"

"Good things come in threes?"

"Huh? I don't know why that should be. But wait a second. Would it be a good thing to stop analysis when there's so much going on? If I ever needed to keep track of what's happening and what I feel about it, now's the time."

"Do you need analysis to keep track? Or are you doing it on your own? It seems to me it goes back to that fundamental feeling of whether you're all right, or whether you're in need of repair. Whether you can pretty much trust yourself to follow the right course, or not."

"Well, coming into this with the big surprise that Grace is pregnant does not exactly fill me with confidence. I mean, I blindsided myself, or she and I both did. And it wasn't like you were picking up any premonitions, either. Not that I've expected you to count my condoms. But this is a bombshell."

"Destructive?"

"No. That's just it, isn't it? It's not destructive. It's constructive. Like what'd you call it, our 'dream of the future'? We're constructing a life together, including this baby. But to get here maybe we both just had to close our eyes in order to jump. And now we're in the river and it's not so bad. We float."

"That's the feeling of trusting yourself?"

"I guess it is. Requiring myself to be omniscient won't get me too far, will it? I'd rather float. Or paddle. Still got to pay attention and steer this thing. We're on a raft, heading downriver. I am excited. This is a good day."

"You've had a few good days, haven't you?"

"When you put it that way, it makes me think they're all good days, because they've led to this one."

"How about when you're having a bad day?"

"One way or another, got to seize the day, I suppose. I'm game."

"So, are you ready to stop analysis?"

"Not just like that, not tomorrow. Besides, it's not stopping analysis when I've got you residing in the mental condo, is it? It's not like I stop watching what I'm doing, or forget the way we talk about things as they come up. But it does start to feel like I maybe don't need to come here in order to do that. Or if I do, I could always come back, right?"

"Of course."

"What do you think? Do you think I'm ready to leave?"

"It may well be. I suggest we sit with it awhile and see what it feels like. Then if it feels right, we could set a termination date a few months down the line to give ourselves time to consolidate and say good-bye."

"That's a long good-bye. Of course, it's been a long hello. You know, I get a surge of missing you, but, at least for now, I also feel ready. Maybe six months?"

"Do we need to decide now?"

"No. I guess I'm just trying a time frame on for size."

"What's it feel like?"

"All right. Then I think how big Grace's belly will be in six months. If all goes as it should. I am elated when I think about this."

"You show it."

"Even without leaping about on the couch and whooping?"

"It's in your voice. Now that you mention it, you have been rather active there on the couch, crossing your legs and waving your hands."

"I've got a body, too. All the better to do things with."

"Which you seem to have done."

"And so much more to do."

"That's our time."

"I'm off and running."

"And one more thing?"

"Yes?"

"Congratulations."

"Thank you. Thanks a lot."

"You're welcome. Be well."

"You always say that, 'Be well.' I guess it works. You, too, be well."

6.

MEMORIES, DREAMS, PERCEPTIONS

REMEMBERING TO FORGET

CURIOUSLY, WHEN I CONSIDER my own direct experience, I am here now without beginning and without end. I have my earliest memory—I was bundled up in blankets being pulled on a sled by my girl-aged aunt, who looked back to find me gone, rolled into a snowbank it turned out, nary a peep, smiling happily in my swaddling—but that earliest memory is confusing as to how much I remember and how much I was told. And that distant vicissitude is when memory began, not, they tell me, when I began. I cannot remember my beginning. And my end, despite its certainty, is, at the moment, queasy speculation. The ghost ship of the dead, my personal *Flying Dutchman,* sails unseen over my horizon. Here and now, I am without end.

Without beginning and without end, I place one word after the next onto the blankness of paper, the space before me. I find myself in the moment of placing, as you do in the moment of tracing the words, one falling after the next from the present into the past. The past is a palace of memory* that gives us a place to stand in the present as moment by moment we fold future into past and momentarily hold past in mind. We mind the time. To hold the world together we must not forget.

Forgetting, then, has this great power. While memory corrals experience into what is known, forgetting is the exit gate in the corral's circling fence that lets what is known become no more. If the gate is left too wide open, a person grows patchy and then is gone despite the body's breathing. Grandmama no longer knows who you are. You cannot find her in her body. Yet the gate must be left at least ajar. Memory's corral has a limit.

There's too much to remember. Remembering everything would be like having a map that covers, on a scale of one-to-one, exactly the territory it represents—like a picture of the world laid over the world itself. Remembering everything would take as much time as the living of the life remembered. Your whole life cannot flash before you at the moment of death, because your whole life would take a lifetime to unreel. And you could never die, because remembering the flashpoint of remembering everything again requires again remembering everything, everything again unreeling from the flashpoint until the flashpoint recurs again, again, again. Forgetting fades memory mercifully, so that I am not caught between time's two facing mirrors. Instead, I live between my forgotten beginning and my final forgetting. Forgetting lets me die.

And forgetting lets me live. I live each day noticing, selecting, cobbling together memories and turnings of attention into my fortified perception of my world and me in it, discrepancies forgotten. Automatically, I forget the extraneous, so that I proceed from this minute to the next sustaining my precious self. I stay I by the selective remembering and forgetting that gives me my past and presents my present. Yet I may forget too much.

My seeming choice is to remember how to hang onto what makes me feel good, and how to avoid what makes me feel bad. Desire lures; aversion repels. Ignorance beckons my laziness. It is easier to forget what seems too hard or irrelevant. Living forgetfully, I forget to remember that pleasures pass, that misfortunes always breach the fort, that nothing lasts. I forget to remember what the Buddha reminds me: that desire, aversion, and ignorance ensnare me. My very clinging to them, thus I am told,* is itself the choice that guarantees suffering. Try to remember. If my motivation is to acquire, hoard, engorge, to harm, despise, humiliate, or to neglect, delude, benumb, then I perpetuate suffering. I must remember.

Yet the Buddha's suggestion goes further, to the subtlety of paradox: I must remember to forget* If I remember to recognize the snares of the world for what they are (no easy task), I remember to forget their allure. This remembering to forget allows a forgetting to remember. When the ship leaves the dock, it floats as free as free-floating attention. Through this subtle forgetting to remember, I may be free, even of myself. To be free of myself is a new frame of mind, confusing to the other frame of diligent rememberer. Free, I can avoid the hollow pretence of humming in smug self-satisfaction as I stroll to my grave, "I Did It My Way." Or I can avoid chest-beating lamentations over "Poor me!" Instead, I have a choice to live (and die) mindfully. No I, no way; nothing to remember, nothing to forget.* I can choose to remember to forget, thereby forgetting to remember, thereby transcending both remembering and forgetting. Thus I am told.

One psychoanalytic writer* muses that people come for analysis when they have forgotten how to forget. They are mired in remembering. Having forgotten how to forget, they cannot simply listen, nor evenly suspend attention's quiet gaze over the passing stream of experience. The world is too much with them. They have no choice.

How much do I actually forget or remember by choice? I still have memorized bits and pieces of schoolday poems, but they are peculiar for their fixity. I have the imperious reminder of my appointment book, telling me from one day to the next what's important to remember. I have what I know: places and people and facts, stories, associations, the daily news, moreover the sprawl of language naming things into the being we share as our human world, the whole great show. I do not choose the show. It comes all at once, a three-ring circus of past, present, and future tailored to each fleeting moment, and it comes with me already in it.*

I find I have already automatically chosen to remember what is relevant to the moment. I arrive an automaton, thrown into a world around me, pre-programmed to find pleasure and avoid pain. The pleasure may merely be to sustain myself long enough to draw another breath; the pain may maximally be the crushing stillness of death. Breath or death. The alternative gets me breathing a little faster.

To Do or To Be?*

Breathing faster, I do what I need to. Food and shelter help. Other people matter, if only selfishly for what they can do for me. I must hold myself together, in the face of things always falling apart,* this moment always mutating anew. Constant maintenance. The doing is endless. Always there is more to do. Always one thing leads to another.

While I busily do what I need to do, things also happen all by themselves, without my doing. Experience flows through and around me all of its own accord. The upwelling moment casts me a memory.* I pause from doing otherwise to be with it.

Once—this was in my early twenties—I was living with my girlfriend in a cave in the Yolla Bolla wilderness area of Northern California. This was a shallow cave hollowed out of the undulating rock at the bend of a river. On the opposite bank was a low cliff, and set back above that was a scree of crumbling rock coming down steeply, perhaps at forty-five degrees from the opposite hilltop. One day (such is youth) I swam over there, managing to keep my boots dry by holding them with one arm above my head. Then wearing only those boots I climbed up the hillside to the edge of the scree. I tested it. With any weight at all it began to avalanche down the hill. I know I weighed the risks. If I fell, at the least I'd be scraped up over my entire body; at the worst, if I really hurt myself, my girlfriend couldn't possibly carry me and we were a difficult day's walk from the nearest logging road. So I stepped out and as the slope gave way under my foot I took the next step and the next, each time placing my weight on the one foot just as the ground under the other foot would have carried me with it into the landslide I was creating below. This stroll across the scree to the safety of the other side had, as you can well imagine, my complete and utter attention.

How foolish. We both might wonder how I calibrated those particular scales on which I was weighing the risks. Were they skewed by some latent suicidal impulse, or by some naïve brash denial of death? Maybe, but what really tilted them towards taking the risk, what stands out for me in retrospect, was the requirement of complete and utter attention. I gave myself no room to slip up. There was no turning back and no stopping. I was focused on sustaining, quite literally, my continuity, while each step crumbled into emptiness.

So absorbing was the doing, step by step, each footfall moment between past and future, that I found myself one-pointedly being wholly there, then. I surrendered to the moment.* Ironically, I forgot about doing. My feet took care of themselves, doing what was needed, let free by an alertness of being. I had found, I suppose, being's saliency, without even knowing what I was hunting for. Once safe on the other side, I tucked my find into memory. I had no need to risk a walk across again. (Cheap thrills I can do without.) Usual doing resumed. I carefully picked my way down to the river. So it was, I seem to remember.

I let go the memory, to fade like a dream as attention wanders. Why came that memory, and not some other? The circumstances of its moment brought it. Karma connects: the actions of previous thoughts created circumstantial consequences. That memory was both a consequence and an action that predicated possibilities for further actions. The memory itself served as a footfall, a place to ground myself, a place temporarily to be. Other memories, perceptions, associations come along, likewise footfalls to the automaticity of my selectional doing. Indeed, they appear and disappear all by themselves. Why focus my attention at all? My attention automatically packages the new into the familiar, saves a few soon-old favorites in memory, and forgets the rest. So might I continue, a product of the circumstances I perpetuate. I react to circumstance. Life lives me.

So might I continue, that is, unless I recall that I have some choice about my automaticity.* Try to remember. My choice is not just what to do next, reactively. Actively, I can turn my attention onto itself. I can attend to my attention's lurching this way and that. I can notice how such doing obscures being. If pleasure and pain do not overly rivet my attention, I may discover in this very moment, as I raise my preoccupied eyes from the splinter in my thumb, a star-filled sky above, space to be.

Like a shooting star, a surprising bit of a decade-old dream flashes past. If I am not otherwise embroiled in getting or avoiding, I might choose to hold the dream, to wonder whether holding the dream is a getting or avoiding, to ponder the dream in what I find is an opening, a space before me, where, if I so choose, the dream may reside or sub-side. Such choosing is not a doing, but a letting be. There is room to free, if only a little, being's next moment, and oneself within it. While one thing and another lead to doing this and that, being stays. Being is the emptiness into which the footfall crumbles, the space of mind around the word on the page. Being is so hard to see because doing fills it up. Doings distract. Try to remember.

Doing obscures being.* How then to obscure the doing, to reveal being?

Psychoanalysis, from this vantage, halts some habit-patterns of cus-tomary doing to glimpse being, and being provides room for choice to do differently. Psychoanalysis rearranges the memory that con-structs the world. As thoughts and feelings arise, conversation exam-ines how one clings to the usual, what one inattentively avoids as usual,* and why, and at what cost. Perhaps there is the remembering anew of what had been forgotten, or the tiresomely remembered seen afresh. Or what was deemed so important may, on reconsideration, seem worth forgetting. While analysis may begin as an effort to get all the mental attic in order, it may end with an appreciation of how well the things in the attic rearrange themselves if only they are let be. The invitation is to trust yourself to be who and how you are, to trust your-self to better yourself. The knit-browed effort to fix it all can subside; gentle acceptance can still the dire demands of perfection and control and shame and fear. Being better requires being. Being allows doing better. Being leads, doing follows.

Although psychoanalysis provides an experience of being repeat-edly, reflectively together with another person through time, its goal is not a radical immersion in being. Psychoanalysis revises, regroups, reconstructs what can be talked about, what can be put into words. A verbal account of *what is* remains an account; the account is not *what is* itself. The story of a life is not that life. The story provides a place to stand, to understand. To step outside the story, to "stand in the spaces,"* is to remember to forget.* The story's footfall place must give way with time, when, eventually, there is no foot to fall, no narrator to tell the story. The story, open as it may be to change, is just another doing of words.

How then to obscure the doing, to reveal being? Let a story try.

Once upon a time—in the fourteenth century of our Common Era, to be precise—there lived in the English midlands a hermit monk.* He devoted his life to the love of God. His was not the active life, concerned with deeds. Instead, he chose to contemplate God's being. Words failed him. Eschewing words, he thought to seek no further for Him by the ingenuity of mind. A cloud of forgetting, he realized, could enshroud the dictates of memory. Likewise, concepts, qualities, and expectations must evaporate in a cloud of unknowing. Left in mind between these two clouds of forgetting and unknowing he found a humble darkness holding the simple thought and blind feeling of being. Empty, silent, still, being is. It is *hic stans* and *nunc stans,* abiding hereness and nowness, without beginning and without end.* Near the end of his life, the simple monk turned again to words to write down for others a description of what he had found. He advised that you think no more of yourself than of God. God is as God is; you are as you are. God and you are "without any separation or disturbance of the mind. He is your being . . ."* The verbal description could not be the experience, but it could be a suggestion of possibility. He did not sign his name to his writing, perhaps because he felt that who he was did not matter.

How then to obscure the doing, to reveal being? Let another story try.

Once upon a time—Thursday, April 25th, 2002, to be precise— there lived another English-born monk,* a Buddhist monk who was trained in the Thai forest tradition of the Theravada, the "Doctrine of the Elders" adhering to the Pali canon, the earliest Buddhist texts. He had been invited to lead a meditation retreat in the countryside of western Massachusetts. Days passed mostly in silence, with alternate periods of sitting and walking meditation. Each day he'd give a talk, spontaneously, about whatever came to mind. What came to mind this Thursday was the practice of "aimless wandering." It requires first, he recounted, a capacity for sustained concentration, of the sort developed through years of practiced focusing of the mind on one thing. The "aimless" variation is to let go the one thing and to extend mindful regard to one thing after another as each arises and passes away. The wood paneling on the wall brings to mind (surprisingly, because forgotten for years) a boyhood afternoon in a summer camp's woodshop; the wall's window gives rise to the notion, then the action, to walk outside. One finds oneself at the confluence, or *as* the confluence, of arising and passing away. One follows and flows with what arises, both outwardly and inwardly, though the outward and inward are hardly different.

As the bird chirps outside my window, so chirps my mind. *My* mind? So chirps mind.

At first this aimless wandering might seem to describe the typical unreflective way of leading life, buffeted between desires and aversions and the least-resistance preference for ignorance as bliss, moving along reactively, doing one thing after the next. But that sort of wandering is egotistically aimed, a grasping at the accumulation of experience in the service of self, like collecting hotel towels from around the world. Aimless wandering is less a grasping than a reflective witnessing of what is through a self-of-the-moment lightly forgotten. This self itself is forming and reforming, ever arising and passing away. Form reveals emptiness; emptiness form. Attention's aimless wandering opens being in one form and another. Nothing need be done.*

How to obscure doing to reveal being? Move between clouds of forgetting and unknowing, between distinctions of outward and inward. See fixity in flux, flux in fixity. Attending needs no attender; perceiving no perceiver; remembering no rememberer. Let yourself go. What is, is. Silent, empty even of itself, being encompasses all.

MULTIPLE BEING

I sit. I close my eyes. I see before me a blankness—though pulsing, if I look carefully, with fading after-images, dim floating blobs, nascent light and subtle shadow. I say, "In the space before me I see a white lotus." From my memory I retrieve the image of a white lotus, floating against an inky black. The lotus is real, the petals soft, cupping inside a starburst of golden pistils. With practiced visualization, I understand, the lotus can become more and more real, less a visualization than the perception I might have of a lotus in a vivid dream. Yet there remains the lotus and me, the observed and the observer. A further reality in mind,* is for me not to see, but to become the lotus.

Visualizing the lotus is a doing; the lotus itself is a being. The leap from doing to being requires letting one self die, as it were, in order to arise anew. While I am the lotus, I am not I. Yet mindfulness can sustain a connection. Mindfulness sustains an attention to attention, an effortless remembering to forget, a holding to holding* rather than to that which is held, and thereby mindfulness spins threads of connection. My being is multiple. Without contradiction I am I, even while I am the lotus. And you are you, and I.

Consider the mycelium of a mushroom, that underground web of threads so thin they can grow interpenetratively between the cells of roots and tree trunks. Like the neuronal network of a brain, the mycelium is a complexly interconnected microscopic matrix. But the brain is small. One living entity, a mycelium can be miles across, its fruiting bodies the mushrooms in this nearby grove, the mushrooms in that far-off place, seemingly different, genetically the same. Perhaps I and the lotus and you are like mushrooms of mycelial being. The problem is how to discern our threads of connection, to recognize in presence of mind our common and multiple being.

Threads of sustained attention, the Tibetans say, can stretch unbroken between waking and dreaming, indeed, from life, beyond death, to life again. Threads cross between me and you. Minding makes visible threads that are there. Look, they suggest, practice, see for yourself.

I do not know. I stumble in the dark. Then across the dark, it may be, I find you. We talk. I hum, out of the blue, "Getting to know you, getting to know all about you." You cannot stand Broadway musicals. I stop humming. We look out for each other's rough edges. What there is about you—your story, your relations, your endeavors—is forever fascinating, not in itself, but because of how and who you are, forever forming, unforming, coming to be. In coming to know your ways of being, I can come to be as you, and you as me. Each of us can be the same, while different; while being neither different, nor the same; while being formed and empty of form, manifesting each of us alike the Buddha within.

TRANSFORMATION

Becoming another requires becoming other than oneself.

On the face of it, this seems impossible. Am I not tethered body and mind, as are you? Are we each not locked into our unique genetic endowments and irreproducible histories and idiosyncratic perceptions? An old and basic premise of interpersonal psychoanalysis assumes an elasticity* between analyst and analysand: where their realities do not overlap, there is a push and a pull between them to determine, anew, the real. The patient begins, perhaps, feeling battered and broken; the analyst begins, perhaps, empathically to feel just how battered, how broken just so. Only the analyst cannot be the patient; empathy at times must fail. The analyst sees the patient as someone other than the patient is. The patient contends with this other patient the analyst implicitly proposes. The other as a way of being intrudes.

Likewise the analyst may well feel other than the patient's perception of who the analyst is. This other, as a mistaken way of being, or as a possible way of being, intrudes.

Each feels misperceived. Each violates the reality of the other. Each marshalls every resource to shore up what's what. Yet, being other, each one can see, in part, what the other cannot.

So gradually, mutually if not equally, realities shift. The grip on the real loosens. What was unformulated,* unthought,* dissociated* joins realities. Reality shifts for each. Each becomes another, other than oneself as one had taken oneself to be. Such is one view of psychoanalytic transformation.

In a sense, the way I might be is a visualization at the beginning of my analysis; at the end that way is a realization. I can *do* visualization. I must *be* realization. The process takes time because of the complexity of ways of being, and because of the need to feel connected, whole and unitary from past to present. I am not the same as the boy I was; nor am I different. Yet each moment transforms me anew. The palace of my mind is a shifting projection of memories, dreams, and perceptions. Its realness requires I let it be, and tinker only carefully with the projector.

Someone lost in madness has lost the real. Dissociation of psychotic proportions fractures reality. Yet might not a capacity for dissociation reveal reality's ruse? It is not that reality is not real, but rather that reality is contingent, impermanent, and mutable. We become responsible for the realities we effect. We do them, not they us. Feelings and thoughts and actions effect—make happen—the world. Yet a revelatory dissociation, in order not to be lost in delusion or trapped in a partial reality, requires what Theseus trailed behind himself to retrace an escape from the labyrinth of the Minotaur: a thread.

One Dutch dreamworker* (a flying Dutchman?) describes a technique of "embodied imagination." Berthe has dreamed of a bull. With her dreamgroup she concentrates on its image. Closer, she witnesses its arched back, powerful horns, sexual force. Closer still, almost touching, hearing, and feeling the air snort in its nostrils, she exclaims she wants to *be* the bull. The dreamworker, knowing Berthe is not trained to lose herself in shamanistic ecstasy, keeps her connected in a double consciousness, aware both of the subjectivity of the bull, and of the bull as Other, not the self who describes the experience. Via mental imagery, the bull is in a world. Via embodied imagination, the world is in the charging bull. The "craft of imagination" is to thread together subjectivities, so that the multiple self-states available to each of us are not lost to one another.

Further, so that as persons each of us is not lost to one another, the sustaining thread that holds my "I" together through time is my human relatedness with "You." Says one analyst, "'Unity' is a shorthand term for the experience of feeling fully in life, and 'life' is the experience of our connection with the rest of humanity."*

The thread between us is an affiliation,* an adoption at least in part of the other's way of being. You hold me in mind, sustaining something of my being; so I hold you. We nod in recognition. We matter to one another. We tell each other who we are, while self-states shift, subjectivities flicker. Objectively, we are smelly bodies, visual impositions. Subjectively, we each hold a world with others alive therein, realizations of being. You are the other I may become, while becoming the other you are.

Your otherness is a gift. Close as we may become, known each to each however deeply, you remain incorrigibly other. Your refusal to be only the same as I think you are, to become only my version of you, means that I am always disarmed, never able to stipulate who you are just so. Whether you are a surprising delight or a vexing annoyance, you keep my world open, unclosed by my certainties. Your otherness does not let me rest. I tell you what's what. You tell me otherwise. We form and reform and form again in the eyes of the other.

It's not just between you and me. As well, with mindful regard of myself, I become other to myself. I see me change, perhaps pompous to fearful to greedy, all dependent on actions and circumstance. My states of self (having a good/bad day) pass from one to the next, form following form. No one of me can stay and rest in perpetuity since my others always goad, transforming me inevitably. I form myself this way and that, form and reform, restive, no me my me for long, each form a prison from which I seek escape to be some other.

> Thus play I in one person many people,
> And none contented . . .
> But whate'er I be,
> Nor I, nor any man that but man is,
> With nothing shall be pleased till he be eased
> With being nothing.*

TRANSCENDENCE

Transformation exchanges forms; transcendence goes beyond. A common epithet of the Buddha, *Tathagata,* means "One Who Has Gone Beyond."* Like you and me, he has a human form; unlike you and me, he, the "Awakened One," sees beyond. His transcendent vision is like the opening in the middle of his forehead of a third eye. Sometimes it is depicted with a daub of paint, or a fleck of gold leaf. Sometimes it is a spiral, suggesting plummeting depth. I have seen it as an eye whose axis runs up and down the forehead instead of across, crossgrain to the ordinary. Once I was startled to see it as a sudden beam of light: set in the forehead of the Buddha statue across a room was a jewel whose facets shot there and here lightbeams. The Buddha's two earthly eyes are half-closed, seeing simultaneously the world out there and the world in mind. Form follows form in transformation. The Buddha's fundamentally undepictable third eye is neither open nor closed, neither out there nor in here, all-seeing from every angle, place, and time, yet empty of sight: formless transcendent.

Like you and me, the Buddha has his human form; like the Buddha whose form we share, we, too, may go beyond. We begin through regard of one another. Look into my eyes; invite me into yours. In each other's eyes we find a third sight, the light of you-in-me and me-in-you. Through regard of one another, we begin transcendence of ourselves.

Transcendence is a singularity, all forms as one, and as well, one none because counting is unbegun. All times one time in no time. If I transcend myself, I am no one, eased with being nothing, as are you, in an ease we share.

Or perhaps we share an uneasy reluctance to risk such being. Transcendence beyond duality, beyond logic, beyond words, beyond even death, inspires bafflement and dread, awe and awfulness, but as well the hope for joyous ecstasy. Without hope for transcendence, without courage to risk beyond, we suffer blindly in the separate prisonhouses of our solitary selves.

Psychoanalytic psychotherapy touches transcendence. It seeks to free the self through hope of finding how better to live. Patient and therapist find hope through one another. The way of the Buddha embraces transcendence. It proffers hope to free the self even of itself, through perceiving in each of us a Buddha within.

This Buddha within needs no particular name, no necessary trappings even of Buddhism, because what we perceive is our shared human hope of finding how better to live. We discover in one another the selfsame longing for peace of mind and heart, for care and healing, for a world set right.

It would seem we might readily agree on what is better until we butt up against our differences. I see it my way, you yours. Our shared longing, we may at last discover, does not obliterate, but transcends differences. My way to live better may differ from yours. Your difference opens to me another assessment of the better. Your otherness matters. The ways we differ are gifts to one another, openings to possibilities of change. Transcending difference, we can live not over and above or conflictually against one another, but with and through each other. We love what matters: each other. To live life better is our common cause.

Transcendence, in fact, is ordinary. Feelings and thoughts and actions make up the world. Ordinarily, we look out for one another without much thought. To be more responsible for feelings and thoughts and actions, to assess their harm and benefit, is to live more with others in mind. By my actions, including the action of turning my attention to this over that, I shape myself, and I shape the world. My actions have consequences attention foresees, and consequences that transcend the foreseeable. I shape the world; I dwell in the world given shape by the actions of others.

My food is grown and brought me by others, my house built by, my clothes sewn by, my words known by, always, others. Others stop their cars so I can cross the street.* Others are ready for me when I am sick, or ready to entertain, to teach, to work, to help or to be helped according to what each and the other needs. Without a thought, so much of the time, we take care of each other. We pay the bills doing as promised, smile at the neighbor, say "Please" and "Thank you," and the world becomes in some small way a better place.

A better place except, of course, for those others left thoughtlessly out. Transcendence is not ordinary enough. Complacency ignores the exploitation of those others. Greed excuses their impoverishment. Hatred justifies their slaughter. By intent or neglect, we may shape or permit a world of the robbed and the robbers, the slaughterers and slaughtered. Minding more widely matters. Those others, too, are longing for the transcendence of right actions. They are not others. We are they.

Your otherness is the same as mine. We are the same in our difference. Look at you, at me, the same while different, sparks of being, flickering sparks each sees in the dark of inexorable forgetting. In the space before me I see you. Each of us, for the other, is a source of the light in the eyes.

PARTING

"So this is it, our last session. Feels strange, but I'm glad of it. Still, I'll miss you."

"I'll miss you, too."

"I was thinking I'd want to sit up for the last time, but then when I came through the door I just wanted to do what came naturally."

"So you lay down."

"Right. Onto the couch. My bed. My rocketship. My flying carpet . . . My raft."

"Where's it taking you?"

"Don't know till I get there . . . I guess if it's a raft that doesn't fit because it leaves you off of it. I mean, if I go floating along here, it's not like I'm alone. You are . . . what? . . . four feet away? Even if I don't say anything, you're still here, along for the ride. We're both on the raft. It's more like this room is the raft, not the couch, and we're on the raft together."

"Hmm."

"Floating along. Over the city. I'll always remember this trip with you. We're Huck and Jim."

"Hmm?"

"Let's see. It's been awhile since I've read Huckleberry Finn.* *But I*

remember one scene where Huck gets separated from the raft, goes adrift in the canoe at night in fog or something, and then when he gets back Jim is all sad and weepy thinking Huck is dead. And Huck plays some sort of trick on him, as if to say, 'Ha ha, gotcha, I'm alive after all!,' and then realizes he's done this horrible thing. Because Jim loves him. So he's ashamed of himself when he realizes how he's hurt Jim's feelings. No, it's not just hurting his feelings. He's ashamed because he's kept thinking of Jim as a slave, like he's beneath him or something. And the thing is Jim is a true friend, a fellow human being just like Huck himself. I think he decides that he's never going to hurt Jim again, if he can help it. At least that's what I remember. Have you read it?"

"What do Huck and Jim on their raft have to do with you and me on ours?"

"Hmm. I don't think I've ever tried to trick you. The being ashamed part doesn't ring a bell."

"So you're Huck and I'm Jim?"

"That's what I was assuming. You mean it could be the other way around? No—are you trying to play a trick on me? Let me think. No, that just doesn't fit for me. I've got to be Huck."

"Separating? Going off in your canoe?"

"That part doesn't feel like it's that important. I mean, obviously I am separating after today's session, but I know where the raft is, and you know, in a general way, that I'm out there and that I know how to get back to the raft if I ever need to. And I suppose you're glad I'm out there, paddling my own canoe."

"I am glad. But you've got to be Huck. I've got to be Jim?"

"Let's see. You are bigger and older, and you tend the raft."

"I'm your slave?"

"First thought is 'Of course not,' but second thought . . . I do pay you. If you add it up over the years, I've paid you quite a lot."

"So I'm your hireling."

"Hireling? What a weird word. Why do you think you chose that one, Doc? But just because I've hired you doesn't mean that you're just a hireling."

"Which suggests you're not just a patient."

"Wait, that's where the shame is. I can feel it. I'm ashamed at having closed myself off for so many years from you—and not just from you, but from everyone. By keeping you the doctor and me the patient it felt safe. Like all I had to do was be dismissive."

"The way Huck treated Jim, before he realized."

"That's right. Before he realized Jim was a real guy. More real than he'd let him be."

"What have you realized, between us?"

"Uh-oh. I feel like I've got to qualify this in a million ways to make it clear what I mean, but maybe it's really pretty simple. I love you. Talk about a weird word, 'love' has got to take the cake. I mean it's not sexual, or parental, or even like a close friend. After all, I hardly know anything about you. You don't tell me about yourself, and I don't ask. All we ever talk about is me. Yet at the same time I do know you. I feel like you've let me know you, even though I don't have a whole lot of information about you. And you know me, maybe better than anyone. Who else do I talk with like this? No one, not even Grace. That's different. But the thing is, like with Grace, I know you love me back, without even needing to ask."

"You're not asking."

"You couldn't answer. Besides, it'd just be words. I know it. There's certainty after all. Maybe it's in your own peculiar worrywort way, but you are there for me. You're not just a doc, Doc."

"Takes two to tango."

"I believe you've said that before."

"I believe I have."

"But what does that mean? You're reminding me to take credit for my part in what's happened."

"What's happened?"

"My opening up, I guess. Being open, more. Realizing you're a real person over there, not someone I can dismiss as just doing your job. It's funny, because of lying on the couch with you behind me, it's not like you're over there, it's like you're up there. When I think of where you are, it's like you're in a little room— I guess it's this room—but it's like an attic room up near the top of my head, where I always know you'll be. Makes for an easy commute."

"It occurs to me, being dismissive towards me, then, is also being dismissive toward a part of yourself?"

"Toward a part of myself? Let's see. No, it's more like I'm being dismissive toward all of myself. I mean, I'm choosing to walk around as the dismisser, which means I don't really engage with anybody and everybody thinks I'm aloof or arrogant or whatever. Which I am. Or was. I mean I can still be that way, but at least now I notice it and can pull out of it. What an awful way that's been to live, so lonely."

"Reminds you of . . . ?"

"'Oh Dad, dear Dad, Mama's hung you in the closet and I'm feeling so sad.'* That's been hard to face: how much I've been like him without even realizing it, with the dismissiveness and all. The apple doesn't fall far from the tree. And Mom probably dismissing him in her own way, just as glad to have him out of the house, leaving her and me together. It's the Southern Gothic childhood I never knew I had!"

"With the choice between being dismissive or being merged, as a way of living."*

"Only not so simple, when you add in that we all did actually love one another and wanted the other two to be happy. Or still do love one another, me and my father. The change in the old boy since the pregnancy I still can't believe. Calling all the time. Offering to help out. To be there."

"You've given him a second chance."

"Without knowing I was doing it, of course. But the thing is, he's taken it, the chance. He's going to become a doting grandfather, who would've guessed? And I'm happy for him. It's nice for us, it's nice for him. Even visiting Grace's parents, softening them up on the idea that this wedding is cause for celebration, not their daughter's public shame. They wouldn't be coming to the wedding if it weren't for him. Maybe its being a civil ceremony makes it easier. There's going to be a lot to work out with them over the years. At least they're coming. That's a good start."

"Yes."

"A good start! I'm getting married in the morning—actually in nine mornings. Is this me? I shake my head to clear it, but it is clear, and I can feel a tingling across my chest. It is me. Father, husband, and paid teacher come September. Who would've guessed this one?"

"I think you guessed, didn't you?"

"That's the strange part, looking back on it. It's not like I had some grand plan I was executing. It's more like I was just willing to risk it, to take a chance, and then one thing leads to another and here I am."

"How do you mean? What did you risk?"

"I risked calling out to Grace that night we met in the middle of the night. You could say, I suppose, that we just lucked out, meeting one another. But that'd be leaving my part of it out again. I had to be ready to call out, to keep her from pedaling away."

"And she had to be ready to hear."

"That's true. There's the luck. Right time and place for both of us."

"What brought you there?"

"Who knows . . . Maybe it was just wandering around, finding my way led there then."

"But you were up and about, at that hour."

"You mean what brought me there literally? My bicycle. And I was on my bicycle because I couldn't sleep."

"Your insomnia—"

"—turned out to be a friend in disguise. Maybe I was waking up to find somebody. Of course, I did, didn't I?"

"And so did she."

"Neither of us quite believing our good fortune. She was as ready as I was . . . We were talking about this when we woke up just this morning—or should I say 'just this noon,' since our schedule doesn't quite match the rest of the world's. Soon enough. We were lying there with the sun coming through that frosted chickenwire glass in the big window by the bed, and I was petting her big belly. We got to talking about how we met, the big clock and all, and the excitement of falling in love. And just how extraordinary one thing leads to another until we find ourselves lying on the bed, me petting her belly, our baby going to be there soon enough, crawling around. I know they don't crawl around when they're just born, but we were thinking then about our baby crawling around on the bed with us and how we'd have to take care the little tyke didn't fall off. Which is like keeping an eye out for bad things happening and helping each other out to make the best of it, whatever comes along. We are in it together. And the baby. We talked about petting the baby's head, and its little hands grabbing our fingers, and oops, should've used a diaper, got to change the sheets. No, fortunately we just rewound that one and went back to the little tyke crawling around in the sunshine with us lying there and watching. Easiest diapering we'll ever have. So I was petting her big belly but she stopped my hand and wanted just to hug. She said she was scared that we couldn't know *what would really happen, ever. I said that scared me, too. So we hugged awhile more, I guess till it tired us out. Then we lay there side by side, with the sun coming in. You know with the frosted glass you can't tell what time it is, from the sun I mean, you can't tell exactly where the sun is. So it made me think, and I said, we didn't need to worry about what might happen because right then we were just floating along in our bed on the sunshine. That's what we did, for what seemed like the longest while. We just lay there, holding hands, floating along. It was great."*

"Sounds lovely."

"But you know as I tell you this? I realize it's another raft, isn't it? Only on that raft it's not like I have to be Huck. It's more of a trade-off. We take turns taking care of one another, taking care of the raft."

"Sounds like the very best way to do it ..."

" ..."

" ..."

"That's our time, isn't it?"

"Yes, that's our time."

"I guess, what'd Huck say, I've got to light out for the territory."

"Travel well."

"Thank you. I'm ready. I will."

"Thank you," said the analyst.

They both stand. The younger man puts his hand forward. They shake hands. The younger man turns, walks to the door in the wall of books, reaches for the polished knob, opens the door, then a second door just beyond, to the waiting room. He turns, smiling, and waves to the older man, who smiles back. The younger man leaves, closing the second door behind him.

The analyst walks to the open door, and closes it. He stretches his arms behind him, yawning, then takes off his suit jacket to hang it on the back of the desk chair. He steps toward the windowed wall, turns off the lamp between the two chairs, and pulls a footstool away from its chair to where, when he sits on it, ankles crossed, spine straight, he can gaze out the windows over the city to the sky.

The sun is just gone, darkness just arriving. In the sky stars variously appear, while in the city various windows light. The necklace lights of bridges clasp dark rivers left and right. Boats ply the waters. His eyes half-close.*

Between the darkening, emptying world and where he sits, the reflection in the windows of his consulting room intervenes. The panes catch the desk lit by its lamp, and the floor lamp's shadowy show of walls to the side, the wall of books behind, a glint from the doorknob. Because no light shines directly between the analyst and the windows, in the reflections he is an absence of light, a silhouette of nothing, a human outline unfilled. Without reflection of his own, behind him nothing shows. He is an absence of reflection, clear space. He does not appear to notice. He does not appear to notice that he does not appear.

Sources and Associations

Epigraph

* P. V

Wandering as a young man I returned to my college town
to visit a friend who was still in school. Crossing the cam-
pus just at dusk I cut through a memorial colonnade—
columns on one side, niches with busts on the other. One
pale marble face caught my eye. I stopped before James
Walker, whose inscribed words about "the source of the
light in the eyes" so struck me as to write them down on
a scrap of paper. Only years later did I find out he had
briefly been president of the college; he was better known
as a Congregational minister famous for his oratory. The
bust was carved without pupils. Its blank eyes posed a paradox: the source of their light was in his words. Or was the
source of their light in my eyes as I read his words?

* P. V

    Another pair of blank eyes are those of Jorge Luis
Borges, the Nobel Laureate in Literature. By the time
(1967–1968) he came to that same colonnaded building
to deliver the Charles Eliot Norton Lectures (Borges,
2000), he was totally blind. He spoke without notes (of
what use are notes to a blind man?), gazing upward
through a yellow fog only he could see (Mihailescu, in
Borges, 2000, p. 147). Yet he had eyes to see the "Cambridge" of his poem (Borges, 1969). The poem, like the
lectures, like oneself, is a necklace of memory, strung out
of nowhere, leading once again, in the end, to nowhere's

yellow fog. I was there when Borges was. I did not go to
hear him speak. Ironically, the tapes of the lectures were
lost until, out of nowhere, like a forgotten memory, they
resurfaced to be published thirty years later. Thirty years
later, I did hear Borges speak.

PREFACE

* P. XIV

The relationship between writer and reader involves no
simple transfer of information, because each of us, partly,
in imagination, must become the other. As the psychoanalyst Thomas Ogden (1994, pp. 1–2) puts it, "Reading
involves a far more intimate form of encounter. You, the
reader, must allow me to occupy you, your thoughts, your
mind, since I have no voice with which to speak other than
yours . . . A third subject is created in the experience of
reading that is not reducible to either writer or reader.
The creation of a third subject . . . is the essence of the
experience of reading, and . . . also at the core of the psychoanalytic experience." You and I, by necessity, can only
surmise one another across the mysterious divide
between our subjectivities.

We read each other's actions and reactions. We come to
know one another through words. We affiliate with those
persons and qualities we like and are like, and as well with
those we pointedly remember to be unlike. So we come
to know ourselves through telling each other who we are.
"The thoughts I unthinkingly choose to pay attention to,
the aspects of the world I choose to regard, the people on
my mind, all these are the moment-by-moment choices
that constitute my ongoing being, my very self. Another
choice . . . is to remember to stop the words and their
occluding spells, however briefly, and so to dwell,
unknown even to myself, in silence . . . Anew, across this
silence I want you to know me, and you name me into

being with your words, and I tell you who you are with mine. By our affiliation with each other, we have a place to be" (Langan, 1999a, p. 79). We hold one another in mind.

CHAPTER 1. ATTENDING WITHIN

* P. 1

These musings on sameness and difference were inspired by the Dalai Lama, who reflected, "In being human, we are all the same. On that level, none of us are strangers . . . The essential thing is that we are all the same in being human—thinking, feeling, and being aware . . . Both you and I seek out what we think will be good for us, and we avoid what we think will harm us . . . in the vast realm of our thoughts and emotions, we need careful analysis to develop clear awareness of what is harmful and what is helpful" (Gyatso, 2002, pp. 4–5). That sort of analysis is not psychoanalysis, yet both sorts of analysis—the karmic and the psychoanalytic—require an inward turning to the play of mind itself. Analysis requires first a letting go of presumptions the better to open to the nature of experience.

* P. 1

Freud put it thus: " . . . the attitude which the analytic physician could most advantageously adopt was to surrender himself to his own unconscious mental activity, in a state of *evenly suspended attention,* to avoid so far as possible reflection and the construction of conscious expectations . . . to catch the drift of the patient's unconscious with his own unconscious"(1923, p. 239; see also Freud, 1912). Freud's advice "to surrender himself" was never imagined to be so extreme as the Buddha's more literal willingness to surrender "self."

* P. 2

No-Self (*anatta,* in Pali) according to early Buddhism is one of three intertwined characteristics of existence, the other two being impermanence *(anicca)* and unsatisfactoriness *(dukkha).* Impermanence, on reflection, is obvious: nothing lasts forever. The desire for permanence gives rise to unsatisfactoriness: beauty fades, pleasures pass. Before I swallow one mouthful of food I am wanting the next. And most unsatisfactory is the passing of body and soul. "No-Self *(Anatta)* means that there is no permanent, unchanging entity in anything animate or inanimate" (Mendis, 1979, pp. 2–3).

* P. 2

The lack of any permanent, unchanging entity, however, seemingly contradicts the Buddhist belief in rebirth. If fundamentally there is no self, who or what is reborn life after life? This doctrinal tension, among others, led to the evolution of the Mahayana schools of Buddhism, which emphasize the entrapping paradoxes inherent in dualism. The *Diamond Sutra,* written perhaps in the second century C.E. and a woodblock copy of which dated to 868 C.E. makes it the world's oldest extant printed book (Mu Soeng, 2000, p. 58), decrees that the dualistic appearances of things in themselves obscure a deeper understanding of the nature of things just as they are. What the Buddha points to, in Mu Soeng's words, is beyond the naming of words and the conceptualization of thought, an "eternal, numinous presence outside the confines of time and space, appearance and disappearance"*(Ibid.,* p. 134). The shift is from the psychological and knowable to the ineffable and mystically experiential. The contradiction between *self* vs. *no-self* yields to a paradoxical clarity allowing both and neither. There is a dissolving of dissolving itself (Langan, 2003a). The sutra concludes,

> So you should view all of the fleeting worlds:
> A star at dawn, a bubble in the stream;
> A flash of lightning in a summer cloud;
> A flickering lamp, a phantom, and a dream.

(Mu Soeng, 2000, p. 155)

Even the Four Noble Truths, first approachable as hypotheses subject to analytic scrutiny, ultimately turn inside out: "Know suffering, although there is nothing to know. Relinquish the causes of misery, although there is nothing to relinquish. Be earnest in pursuit of cessation, although there is nothing to cease. Practice the means of cessation, although there is nothing to practice" (Gyatso, p. 4, in Gyatso and Sheng-yen, 1999). The teachings are like a raft to help cross a river; there is no need for the raft once the river is crossed.

* P. 3

In contrast, early Freudian psychoanalysis made no claim to allay the "common misery of mankind," only, in successful cases, to allay the added burden of neurotic suffering. Neurosis was a problem in *knowing*. Interpretation made knowable those truths denied or forfended from consciousness.

* P. 3

My fanciful case of the beautiful baroness demonstrates the psychoanalytic process as an expansion of knowing. Many of Freud's case studies can be read in the same way, as Sherlock Holmesian revelations of darker truths. Always, implicitly if not explicitly, there lurks the certainty that the truth is there to be known.

* P. 4

Contemporary psychoanalysis tends more modestly to acknowledge that what can be known is forever partial and provisional. That modesty reveals a radical shift from a positivist to a constructivist epistemology, from a modern to a post-modern sensibility. So Levenson (1972, 1983) espies a "fallacy of understanding" and an "ambiguity of change." Greenberg and Mitchell (1983) contrast the earlier drive-dominated with the later relationally-oriented turn in psychoanalysis, leading "beyond Œdipus" (Greenberg, 1991) to persons considered in intersubjective relationality (Mitchell, 2000). Pizer (1998) negotiates inevitable clinical paradox, while Stern (1997) navigates the flux between formulated and unformulated experience. Hoffman (1998) develops a dialectical-constructivist view of ritual and spontaneity in the psychoanalytic process. Bromberg (1998) fractionates the unitary self into multiple self-states, between which opens the space where one is no one. These theorists are but a few of many.

Psychoanalysis remains a pursuit of truth, but the truths pursued are partial, altering in context and circumstance. They are less the givens of experience than they are captured bits and pieces, arranged more or less consciously into the mosaic of a person's reality. In R.D. Laing's terms, they are less *data* than *capta,* less things *given* than things *taken* (quoted in Gergen, 1991, p. 89). This view entails an ethical truth: One is responsible for one's choices. Limiting what one pays attention to out of aversion or attachment fosters an ignorance for which one is

* P. 5

responsible. The philosopher Mikhail Bakhtin (Clark & Holquist, 1984) styled this *answerability.* One can go puling or proud before the final firing squad; inescapable is answerability for one's actions. This view, of course, coincides with the karmic understanding of cause and effect, and responsibility for right actions.

* P. 6

The Theravadan monk Ajahn Sucitto (2001, p. 6) reflects that this sort of responsibility is not a matter of picking and choosing so much as an allowing. When the "convention" of personality unfolds into energetic patterns, no "I" is grasped. Acting is freed for the better. Sim-

* P. 7

ilarly, the letting-go process of psychoanalytic change allows a paradoxical changing while staying the same, the illusion of being one self while in fact being many

* P. 7

(Bromberg, 1998). The psychiatrist H.S. Sullivan (1953) proposed that people vacillate between security and satisfaction, i.e., between the safety of staying the same and the risk of embracing change. From a Buddhist perspective, of course, staying the same is a delusion: Everything, always and ever, is changing. The experiencer is merely a changing aspect of experiencing, perceivable as such when one,

* P. 10

so to speak, steps outside oneself. Psychoanalysis, too,

requires a mental sidestep to that vantage outside oneself belonging neither to analyst nor analysand, yet to
both (called the "analytic third" by Ogden, 1994). That
subtle vantage frees the experiencer to the open flow of
experiencing.

*P. 11   Avoided is the infinite regression of a "Cartesian the-
atre" (Dennett, 1991) whereby a homunculus within
organizes sensory experience into a unified whole—but
that inner "I" in turn requires a homunculus within, and
so and on forever.

Typically, and by usual consensus sanely, we take for
granted the reality out there which we in here with our
minds observe. Our capacity to imbue experience with
reality is so automatic as to pass unobserved. Yet that
capacity reveals itself in our ability to take for real (for a
*P. 12   time being) works of fiction and theatre. As Coleridge
(1817) famously put it, "[We] transfer from our inward
nature a human interest and a semblance to truth
sufficient to procure for these shadows of imagination that
willing suspension of disbelief for the moment, which
constitutes poetic faith." The suggestion of the Buddha is
that one's usual reality of self-in-the-world ensues something like a thoughtless suspension of disbelief. Willing
mindful attention reveals the play for what it is.

The Consulting Room

*P. 13   The analytic case backstitched through the regular chap-
ters of this book is fictional, as may become obvious when
the particular themes that come up show an uncanny sym-
pathy with their adjacent chapters. The analysand is not
modeled on a particular person; the analyst is my cousin
thrice-removed in a parallel universe. The fictional
attempt is to demonstrate how turnings of attention can
occur in a psychoanalysis.

Shifting from the one sort of writing to the other requires a turning of attention on the part of the reader which, I hope, can impart something of a mindful self-awareness to the process of reading.

I have borrowed the literary device of interlarded italicized passages from James Agee's (1957) novel, *A Death in the Family*. The book deals sensitively with familial relationships and the loss of a father, as happened in Agee's own life. In real life, as a schoolboy Agee found a different sort of father by proxy in an Episcopalian priest, Father Flye, with whom he maintained a lifelong correspondence (Flye, 1971). That relationship bears comparison with the relationship between analyst and analysand, all in the context of wider relationships mentioned and unmentioned. I mention Agee as an influential ghost behind the text. He influenced me as a schoolboy, where he had walked before my time at our same school, and he walks still, a presence in memory, a living relationship.

As the fictional analyst and analysand assume a presence in the narrative, they make and take a place in the consulting room. The analyst's initial question, "Where are you?," does not, of course, refer to that room. Years ago, the analyst Rollo May (May et al., 1958) mused as to why he would so frequently begin a session with this question. It was because in an important way he did not know whether the patient was far or close, coming or going in relationship to him. It was as if the place they found themselves might be hot or cold, still or roiled, easeful or not. His room was not defining. They had yet to define their room.

Likewise, between the fictional analyst and patient, the thrust of the dialogue is not to come up with whys and wherefores, or with explanatory interpretations. The effort is to describe the nature of their experience, to turn deepening attention to the passing flow of experience.

* P. 14

* P. 17

Describing what it was like for the patient to do his laps in the park was to discover himself at a motionless dead end incarcerated by anger and frustration. He found that place around him in the room where he lay on the couch. He found as well a turning, a way out, changing the room to a place fondly shared for another while. All along, it had been that place, too, but not until noticed. The fixity of place, like the fixity of self, cannot be assumed.

And this explanation of what the two of them were doing in that malleable room is plausible in hindsight, but is merely one account of many possible accounts of what was going on. By another, more Buddhistic account, clinging yielded to a letting go, anger to compassion, denial to greater wisdom. The clinging was to a self-inflicted way of being. The analyst's staunch companionship reflected compassion. The patient's second thought revealing his truer feelings towards the analyst permitted some small measure of wisdom. So things change, for the better.

CHAPTER 2. FINDING EMPTINESS

* P. 19

Central to Mahayana Buddhism is the paradox that "emptiness is not other than form, form too is not other than emptiness"(Gyatso, 2002, p. 60). A paradox by definition is unsolvable yet I find myself in an effort at translation bouncing between the one term and the other. How is emptiness form? I am like the father of a boyhood friend, who had clambered between a small boat and its trailer to secure it. When a fleck of paint fell towards his eye, he jerked his head back, banging it on the axle of the trailer. Rebounding from the bang, he cracked his forehead onto the boat. Rebounding from the boat—you get the picture. He did manage to stop, and feebly joked that it was lucky he was wearing a hat. I suppose I am wearing my thinking cap.

* P. 19   Visualization as a meditative practice in Tibetan Buddhism (see, in particular, Blofeld, 1970) centralizes the paradox of emptiness and form. First emptying the mind, the meditator visualizes one thing, which may change into another, or may become part of a complex panoply of interconnected imagery. The visualization of White Tara (Gehlek, 2003), a bodhisattva manifesting healing and compassion, begins "in the space before me" where appears a white lotus, atop which comes a moon cushion, whereon rests a syllable that becomes a flower that becomes in turn the goddess, who is visualized in greater and greater detail, returning, in the end, to emptiness. [A more detailed rendition is in Langan (2003b); Lopez (1997) presents a scholarly review of the various Taras in Tibetan soteriology.] Calling such a meditative practice visualization is, however, something of a misnomer, since it leads more to ontogeny, the creation of a living being. Tara, for example, is more than a picture in the mind's eye: she is a living embodiment generating into the universe around her compassion, healing, and life-mending power.

Her form is emptiness, emptiness formed, embodied * P. 20 light, in the same universe where "such small beings as we/ travel in the dark" (Strand, 1978). Where I am and what forms where depend on what I attend to. Yet, * P. 21 according to Chang's (1977, p. 8, fn. 2) "relative, flowing, undefinable, and ungraspable nature of all things" all wheres and whats, understood correctly, are empty.

* P. 22   Western physics (per Hawking, 1988, 2001; Greene, 1999) describes a universe uncannily congenial with a Buddhist view of things (Mu Soeng, 1991, 2000). Space is * P. 24 time, time is space in space-time (Hawking, 1988, esp. pp. * P. 25 25–30). Space and time began with the Big Bang from a point containing all points (like the "aleph" of Borges, 1949), a singularity, a point before points, no point in itself (Greene, 1999, p. 346).

* P. 25
Avalokiteshvara's speech in the Heart Sutra (Gyatso, 2002, p. 60) describes the relation of emptiness and form as itself a singularity, the abolition of duality. Rightly
* P. 25
understood, form manifests emptiness (*Ibid.*, p. 116).

* P. 27
What, then, is this form I call myself? Almost three centuries ago the Scottish philosopher David Hume (1739) arrived at a conclusion similar to the Buddha's: "For my part, when I enter most intimately into what I call *myself,* I always stumble onto some particular perception or other ... I never can catch *myself* at any time without a perception, and never can observe anything but the perception ... I may venture to affirm of the rest of mankind, that they are nothing but a bundle or collection of different perceptions, which succeed each other with an inconceivable rapidity, and are in perpetual flux and movement" (p. 300). This form I call myself is a play of shifting forms.

* P. 27
This play of shifting forms is quite the opposite of the *cri de guerre* of the British Victorian poet William Ernest Henley, who in his poem "Invictus" declared, "Out of the night that covers me/ Black as the Pit from pole to pole/ I thank whatever gods may be/ For my unconquerable soul." His is one form, one self-state of wrathful determi-
* P. 27
nation. Available, too, one hopes, are such meditative self-states as those described by Jack Engler (2004) which include the capacity for being lovingly heart-centered.

* P. 29
That heart-centered openness finds words through Peter Matthiessen's (1978, p. 212) *cri de cœur,* "I ring with life ... there is a ringing that we share. I understand all this, not in my mind but in my heart ..." The form of the cry "I exist" begins to matter less than the fact of space, emptiness, room to exist. The psychoanalytic analogy of
* P. 30
standing in the spaces (Bromberg, 1998, p. 186) becomes a capacity to let oneself go in order to let onself be anew, moment by moment. To agree with Borges
* P. 31
(1969) that "behind the face that looks at us there is no

* P. 31

one" is no horror of loss, but rather the freedom to be. C.J. Jung (1961) autobiographically accounted himself a heap of "memories, dreams, reflections." The reflections are illusory if there is no one to reflect. Instead, each of us becomes a kaleidoscopic turning of memories, dreams, perceptions.

Opening

* P. 33

When the patient says to the analyst, "You're trying to tell me you don't run around worrying about these things?" and then takes the accusation back, the interchange touches on the careful and mostly unconscious regulation of anxiety between the two of them (Bromberg, 2003a). The bald accusation could well raise the analyst's anxiety in that it draws into awareness an implicit and comforting stance of being holier-than-thou in regard to the patient. Some part of the patient mistrusts that postured holiness, yet is reluctant to confront the analyst about the analyst's image of himself he seems to need to hang onto. At base, both analyst and analysand speak from within roles adopted to define their relationship. The adopted roles reduce anxiety inasmuch as they provide defined expectations; they also permit using roles to undo roles, an anxiety-laden undertaking whereby each party can see himself and the other anew. From the new viewpoint, past strategies to make oneself feel better or at least familiarly oneself might seem pathetic or shameful. How dare the analyst assume the stance of guru! Likewise, how dare the analysand assume the diehard stance of longsuffering martyr! Instead, each is faced equally with the necessity of humility (Weber, 2004). Each, because of his strategies to reduce anxiety as well as despite those strategies, must come to the conclusion that "We are all simply more human than otherwise" (Sullivan, 1953).

* P. 34   When the analyst comments that the patient is in "the same old fix: wishing that someone can do it for you" and that he "didn't get enough of those apron strings," the patient might well suspect in a half-thought way that the analyst is retaliating critically in response to the patient's feint at puncturing the analyst's worry-free pretention. There is a kind of dance. Each colludes with the other to be accepted all right as is, and to be taken and used and known as an old familiar (Fairbairn, 1958); at the same time, confrontationally and somewhat painfully, as if stepping on one another's toes, each helps the other to break out of old patterns of self-regard and of regard of the other.

The relative anonymity of the analyst can interject into the analytic situation an openness: the analyst is "other" with many blanks not filled in. Just as it is a developmental task for the child to recognize the mother not as a puppet of the child's desire but as a separate other, an agent of her own and otherly desire, a similar task occurs during psychoanalysis (Benjamin, 1988). The analyst can be other than assumed, and likewise can the analysand. Confrontation with otherness permits becoming other than one shopworn self. Confrontation with otherness, as well, poses an in-your-face ethical dilemma (Levinas, 1999): responsibility for how one affects the other (and one's own otherness) through action and inaction.

* P. 36   Responsibility for choice of action is no simple rational proposition. Farber (1966) distinguishes two sorts of choice, two realms of the will (discussed also on p. 46 ff. in relation to mindfulness). The first is the familiarly simple: Shall I go here or there? Order the chocolate or the vanilla? The second taps a deeper current, entailing less a choice than a yielding. So one allows oneself to fall asleep, or more broadly, to be the way conditions (internal and external) call for. Via that second realm, a poet might look

back across her life and discern an inevitability towards becoming a poet despite the wrong turns and contrary aspirations of the past. The deeper choice is toward harmonizing oneself with others in the world, toward a way of being that provides some measure of vocation, purpose, and meaning.

* P. 38

When the analyst and patient joke about time at the end of the session, their wordplay albeit verbal is nonetheless play, a harmonizing give and take rendering them, for the time being, playmates in a relationship that matters.

CHAPTER 3. CONSCIOUSNESS

* P. 41

Gerald Edelman and Giulio Tononi (2000, pp. 113–156; also Edelman, 2004) propose the dynamic core hypothesis as a brilliant explanation of how matter becomes mind. Neurons are not repositories of information, but contributors to a transcendent patterning much in the way logs sustain a fire. Consciousness is like the fire that arises from

* P. 42

innumerable neuronal firings. By extension, character (Piers, 2000) is a perduring pattern of self-organizing complexity.

Yet because by this hypothesis the brain speaks mostly to itself, the model stops short of the more radical interaction suggested by "the Buddhist metaphor of Indra's net, where every being is like a mirror at each point in a vast, dynamic web, reflecting and containing all the other points . . . [Between two people, a] living, vibrating emotional field takes shape [and] stimulates the growth of neural connections in the brain essential for affective life and creative thinking" (Bobrow, 2003, pp. 210–211, in

* P. 43

Safran, 2003). For Buddhism, awareness of the perceived and perceiving gives rise to the constructed experience of being an individual perceiver (Olendzki, 2002, p. 13; 2004b). But further, in our interconnectedness and interchangeability we are each like a neuron in a wider, overarching, transcendent web of sentient being—the bare being, perhaps, of enlightenment.

Various authors describe various aspects of what might be considered a transpersonal sentience available to all.

* P. 44 The Dalai Lama (Gyatso, 2002, pp. 25–29) provides an overview of the thirty-seven aspects of the path to enlight-
* P. 45 enment. Olendzky (2002, 2004a) explicates the four
* P. 45 foundations of mindfulness. Freud's (1912, 1923) comments on "evenly suspended attention" are quoted in the
* P. 46 note to *P. 1. Fenton (2003) describes Daudet's self-
* P. 46 perceived affliction in being *homo duplex*. Farber's (1966) realms of the will, elaborated in the note to *P. 36, contrast busy choosing with a more choiceless awareness. Phillips (1994, p. 32) muses, "It is almost as though Freud is saying that [people] already have something like an analyst inside them, 'simply listening'; and that a person comes for analysis when this inner analyst can no longer sustain evenly suspended attention. That this internal figure has forgotten how to forget." The "analyst inside" bears comparison to the "Buddha within" each of us is
* P. 50 assumed to share. The "analytic attutude" (Schafer, 1983), like mindfulness, attempts simply to turn attention to what is.

Good Day, Good Night

* P. 55 When the analyst asserts, "And you were a weird kid," his statement might be an attack, or ironically, a compliment. Or it might be both. It depends on whether the weirdness is a quality that makes the patient different from, and so rejectable by, the analyst; or whether the weirdness reveals courage on the patient's part to be himself in the face of pressure towards conformity. The analyst could value if not share that courage. Complication arises

because the statement is indeed an attack when the patient is feeling interpersonally abandoned, and indeed a compliment when the patient is feeling affirmed, and unconsciously he can feel both ways simultaneously without contradiction. Accordingly, the problem posed is how to remain open to either possibility and neither, which requires an increasing degree of comfort with paradoxical indeterminancy.

* P. 56
Fromm (1941) wrote about "escape from freedom" as a resort to an authoritarian conformity in order to avoid more difficult problems of personal choice and responsibility. Weiss and Samson (1986) considered the process of psychoanalysis an escape from the directives of tyrannical unconscious beliefs towards a similar freedom of greater

* P. 58
personal choice and responsibility. When the patient considers his relational stance as an unconscious mode of communication—his depression as a link to being with and like his mother—he moves towards a greater freedom of choice in how to be.

* P. 59
One way of looking at the analytic situation is that it frees up, for both parties, a fluidity in moving between modes of being I, Thou, and Other (Langan, 1995). My "I," my most private experience of being myself, is incommunicable. I may tell you about that experience, but I can never convey it to you, as it were, from the inside out. My "Other" (on the other hand) is objective: my body, actions, words, the roles I take, my biographical details, the dry husk of my obituary. Between the two is my *Thou* in relation to yours, our reciprocal sense of the possibilities of each other's being. Having relatively little objective information about the analyst can better open the relationship to an *I-Thou* way of knowing (Buber, 1923). The

* P. 60
analyst's query as to whether he is learning to be "weird" like the patient might suggest, in this context, an appreciation of *Thou,* the patient's way of being.

* P. 61

The name "Grace" (whose felicitous associations were once brought to my attention by Dr. Emily Garrod) describes, to my way of thinking, a central feature of *I-Thou* relationship: an honoring of the presence of another.

CHAPTER 4. MYSTERIES BETWEEN

* P. 63

The quotation is the first verse of a poem by Mark Strand (1964) which concludes, "We all have reasons/ for moving./ I move/ to keep things whole." Presence requires removal; absence, presence. *To be* requires in metaphysical symmetry *to be not*.

* P. 65

Children learn a singsong rhyme: "Hickory dickory dock/ The mouse ran up the clock/ The clock struck one/ And down he come/ Hickory dickory dock." It strikes me that all unknowingly they sing the knell of death. Likewise, in the grim words of lullaby, "When the bough breaks/ The cradle will fall/ And down will come baby/ Cradle and all." We find ourselves between limits, faced by turning points.

* P. 65

Robert Thurman's (1994) discussion of betweens in Tibetan Buddhism as I present it here may lend itself too readily to an interpretation that a lasting "I" travels through time from one self state to another, from one life to another life reborn, much like Christianity's eternal soul. The Buddhist conception, as I understand it, is subtler: though a flame may pass from one candle to another, it both is and is not the same flame. Further, who "I" am is utterly dependent on my condition, that is, on the defining limits of my between-state. Who I am in a particular dream and on a particular day may be very different, though lent some continuity by memory. Memory makes me the protagonist of my story (Schafer, 1992). When memory changes, memory changes me. Memory sets the horizon of my world.

* p. 66
Meditation or meditative states of consciousness (Goldstein & Kornfield, 1987; Rosenberg, 1998) may help reveal and pry apart the circling line of horizon that * p. 67 limits a world to itself. So found Silberer (1909, 1912), able to sustain a thread through his hypnagogic imagery to wander from the confines of the day to dreamworld. So * p. 68 find the Tibetans (Varela, 1997; Norbu, 2002), discerning * p. 68 with lucidity an available path. So finds the Dutch psycho-analyst Robert Bosnak (1996), who espies "tracks in the wilderness of dreaming."

* p. 68
The relation of waking and dream states, of conscious and unconscious mind, is similarly understood in Tibetan Buddhism and in psychoanalysis. According to the Dalai Lama, "First of all, within Tibetan Buddhism, you can speak of manifest versus latent states of consciousness. Beyond that, you can speak of latent propensities, or imprints . . . These are stored in the mind as a result of one's previous behavior and experience . . . during the daytime one accumulates some of the latent propensities through one's behavior and experiences, and these imprints that are stored in the mental continuum can be aroused, or made manifest, in dreams. This provides a relationship between daytime experience and dreams. There are certain types of latent propensities that can manifest in different ways, for example by affecting one's behavior, but they cannot be consciously recalled" (Varela, 1997, p. 79).

Indeed, Francisco Varela, himself a neuroscientist, considers dreaming "a fundamental cognitive activity . . . where people can engage in imaginary play, trying out different scenarios, learning new possibilities; a space of innovation where new patterns and associations can arise, where whatever was experienced can be elabo-rated. This is quite close to some views in psychoanaly-sis" (Ibid., p. 35).

This is quite close to a theory of "oneiric Darwinism" elaborated by the psychoanalyst Mark Blechner (2001, esp. pp. 76–79). He posits that during nightly dreaming the mind permits relatively random variations and mutations of memories, percepts, words, and concepts. Useful new thoughts are retained in memory, useless rejected, and all the while dreams need not be consciously remembered to have a productive effect on waking thought. In coming to a creative solution to a workaday problem, for example, a useful turn of mind will find its use.

Such a view, however, is logocentric, in the sense of being biased towards the rationality of waking consciousness. For the Tibetans, waking and sleeping are interconnected yet separate *bardo* realms of existence. The relation between waking and dreaming is more a two-way arrow. Perhaps the function of waking is to elaborate who and how I may be in my dreams. The lucid dreamer is not dreaming to live life while awake, but, with preternatural agency and choice, is living life while asleep.

Yet the problem of identity in transition from one realm to another remains. How can some essential self transit from one realm to another when each realm defines the terms of what self is? Any one reality seemingly accounts for everything necessary to be real, and this applies not just to the realms of sleeping and waking, to the realms between death and rebirth, and to the six realms of rebirth (human, animal, etc.) Epstein (1995) recounts and reconstrues as psychological modes of being human. Who is reborn? Holding to an essential self suggests one impermeable and eternal—as well as portable —reality: my "I."

Buddhism's doctrine of no-self denies that essentialism. So does, in fact, Kurt Gödel's 1931 Theorem of Incompleteness, which implies that my consciousness in its own terms of reality cannot prove as true or false such

* P. 70

* P. 70

logic-stoppers as the Cretan paradox. The Cretan Epime-
dides avows, "I am lying." If so, his statement is false; if
false, his statement is true. Truth and falsity, reality and
unreality, are artifactual to their limiting constraints.

Likewise, Edwin Abbott's (1884) mathematical
romance of *Flatland* underscores the inevitable necessity
of interdimensional escape. The consciousness of a resident of no-dimensional Pointland knows neither extension nor change (perfect singularity?). Transposed to
Lineland, he knows the one dimension of forward and
back. Coming round a circle to find himself incompre-
hensibly where he began, recognition dawns as to the
criss-crossable two dimensions of Flatland. Crossing (like
Magellan) Flatland's edge of the earth to arrive home
again forces upon him his existence in Spaceland: up and
down join the points of his compass. And obviously, three
dimensions cannot ultimately suffice.

The resident of Flatland contends with a few countable
dimensions. Each human being, alive to each moment,
contends with dimensions innumerable.

Between dimensions Benoit Mandelbrot (1983) inter-
jects fractal geometry. While two-dimensional geometry
proves adequate to describe the relationships of lines and
shapes on a plane, crumpling up the paper on which the
figures are drawn requires a three-dimensional description.
Flatten the paper out, and the description is less three- than
two-dimensional. Required is a geometry of the between.
There is an indeterminate gap between dimensions, a prob-
ablistic indeterminacy, wherein patterns recur, self-similar
but never the same, at smaller and smaller degrees of reso-
lution. So the whole head of cauliflower resembles one of
its florets looked at up close, each floret stemlet in turn
resembling the larger wholes. Yet the repetitive self-similar
pattern is no essential continuity, but an artifact of its gen-
erative terms, an incident of cauliflowering.

By extension to the multidimensionality of moment-by-moment human being, the track between coherently dimensional states of being (e.g., dreaming, waking—cauliflowering?) must pass through an interdimensional no-man's-land—in psychoanalytic terms, through a barrier of dissociation. But on either side of that barrier, certain "latent propensities" imprint and constrain (karma-like) the possibilities of self-experience, rendering the reborn self-similar (but never identical) to the previously-born. A propensity to pass through barriers without dissociating strengthens with barriers crossed. Dissociation lessens. Self extends itself between dimensional self-states.

Though while awake I am no longer who I was while asleep, I can recognize myself. I am not a cauliflower. Nonetheless, if I turn my wakeful gaze inward, the unidimensional coherence of my self begins to erode. Perhaps a cauliflower I may yet become.

* P. 72

The Enlightenment encyclopædist Denis Diderot (Hampshire, 1993) likened his introspectively regarded self to a swarm of bees, the reconfiguring patterns of his thoughts and feelings. (Like the "strange attractors" of chaos theory, coherent patterns arise from incoherent underlying actions.) Diderot's metaphor carries well the shifting patterns of multi-dimensionality in the experience of self, except that bees might become stars, stars flakes of flurried snow, snow grains of sand, tossed sand rippling rings of water, subsiding to emptiness. Looking inward reveals "Who am I?" to be no simple question.

Mandlebrot began with a simple question: How long is the coastline of Great Britain? Hunting up an answer in an atlas is no fair, not because an approximation of the coastline at mean high tide cannot be made, but because an approximation is an imaginary assumption of a unitary dimension where none exists. Look hard at the real world.

Waters lap the shore, always in motion. Even if we freeze the coast at a moment in time (and where are the edges of a moment?) no line appears. Do we trace the rivers inland? Where does the water stop and the land begin? We look more closely, trying to find the edge of the sea's foamy tongue against the sandy shore. Even at the molecular level we find a perpetual indeterminacy: more or less sea or sand always intermingle. No clearly demarcating line ever appears.

Who am I? Where is the line where I stop and you begin? In contemporary psychoanalysis long-assumed unidimensional entities erode. One such is gender, becoming soft (Harris, 2005). One is the distinction between self and other, blurring into an "analytic third" (Ogden, 1994). Another is self itself (Bromberg, 1998; Langan, 1999b).

Another is the text of this book. The wash of the first chapters carries burrs of asterisks (like intersections in Flatland), which lead to these very "Sources and Associations"—not, as it turns out, a collection of footnotes but a text in itself. Should there be another set of alternative asterisks (‡?) leading to yet another text, another associational layer? Or, like the Dalai Lama's "latent propensities," is there another such set already, as yet unseen? Looked at closely enough, everything begins to dissolve. Let us hold hands while we may.

In this shape-shifting world, from the locus of each shape-shifting self, arises the recognition that we can hold each other as companions well-met, not alone, but joined in compassion to "let us be true to one another" (Matthew Arnold, from "Dover Beach"). Hatred hurts all; affiliation (Langan, 1999a) heals. A Buddhist sensibility (Batchelor, 1983) suggests that we can existentially find ourselves being not merely alone with others in a meaningless world of despair, but through being *for* others transcend that world to find unimagined freedom.

* P. 74

* P. 74

* P. 75

Babies

* P. 77   The book seemingly supported by the analysand's toes, *Irrational Despair,* can be found as the penultimate entry on the bookshelves of this book's bibliography. How it got there requires finding a lost track through several realities.

* P. 77   Realities shift. When the analysand recalls in passing the bicycling with his girlfriend along the riverpath, he could pause more fully to remember: *Bicycle wheels spinning beneath them in the dark they sailed up the black asphalt path alongside the riverbank, sailed through electric light and night shadow, wheels whishing, to their left a sparkle-lit tugboat, barge a-tow, churning downstream foaming bow cutting the river; to their right the city, its high hum, its glittering skyscrapers' stockade. They pedaled apace, side by side, glanced about, glad for the ride; one and another caught light in their eyes together. The air, soft rush, made way. Side by side as one they sailed in wind, they whooshed in sound, in mind they flew.*

* P. 83   In reality, the recipe for croissants (for which I thank Ms. Krystin Rubin of the Bread and Butter Bakery, Boston) works prize-winningly well. No doubt the quantities of the ingredients need alteration for home use.

CHAPTER 5. ATTACHMENTS

* P. 85   William James's (1902) averring other forms of consciousness, separated from waking consciousness "by the flimsiest of screens" (from his *Varieties of Religious Experience;* quoted by Obeyesekere, 2004, p. 7) downplays the adhesive seductiveness of the screen of waking consciousness. After all, on the screen of waking consciousness there plays out for all of us the stories of our lives, with all their yearnings, fears, glories, and failures. From a Buddhist perspective this high drama does matter, but not in the way the naïve protagonist might think. Actions make a difference, for better and for worse. What is better, however, is not necessarily that the story of my life have my own happy ending; what is better is that I recognize it fundamentally as a story. It is a story brought about by inconceivably numerous past actions and events, and a story to which I importantly contribute through the actions I take now, and for which I am unavoidably responsible. Yet it is a story projected on "the flimsiest of screens."

I remember at age five one morning strapping on my cap pistol in its holster, donning my Wild Bill Hickok fringed jacket, my blue bandanna neckerchief and my red cowboy hat, and why I remember that morning is because I managed to play cowboy, never forgetting I was a cowboy, all day. At the end of the day my mother persuaded me to remove my outfit and settle down for the evening by her offer of a bowl of warm noodles with butter and salt and pepper and I think a few peas (tuna casserole *in statu nascendi*). It was a relief to stop the play. The noodles were superb. Might such a relief await me still?

The Buddha found relief through the renunciation of play. His determination was to see clearly what is. Whereas Descartes (1637), with the same determination, looked inward to proclaim *"I think, therefore I am,"* the Buddha, so to speak, more subtly recognized "I think I am."

* P. 87

Descartes set the stage for a mind/body dualism that would permeate Western philosophy for the next three centuries: the thinking subject examines the objects of the world. Yet a problem as to *what is* inheres. Looking out from the window of the inn where he wrote, Descartes could only see the hats of passersby. He realized he could in no way see their minds. They could be what later philosophy, in an ineffective struggle to lay them to rest, named zombies (Dennett, 1991; Edelman & Tononi, 2000; Hunt, 1995; Searle, 1992). If I cannot see your mind, how can I know you have one?

The Buddha did not base *what is* in the dualistic thinking of waking consciousness. "I think I am" implies that I am like a byproduct of thinking, like smoke from a circumstantial fire; no thinking, then no I. Mind is not yours and mine. You and I are of a mind. Mind subtends thinking. Awakened mind, an empty clarity, is.

* P. 88

Accordingly, in the story of the Buddha's quest, it is significant that at the moment of enlightenment under the Bodhi tree he did not cry "I am liberated," but "It is liberated!"(Armstrong, 2001, p. 85, per the *Majjhima Nikaya*, 36). His awakening transcended self, unbound the constraints of egotism. Emphasizing the importance of awakening to no-self, Obeyeskere (2004) finds parallels in the Nietzschean contrast between "it" and "I" thinking; in James's stylization of mystical states as ineffable, noetically profound, transient, and passively beheld; and in postmodernism's deconstructive forays.

So I lay down my cowboy outfit, and there are my noodles. More importantly, there is my mother, who makes me warm noodles. Like the enticing taste of the butter on my tongue, says the Buddha, even this bond between parent and child must be renounced lest it obscure *what is*. In his quest for enlightenment, after naming his newborn son "Rahula," which means "Fetter," he leaves him behind (Obeyesekere, 2004, p. 8).

* P. 88

His treatment of his son and wife upon his return, according to legend (as recounted by Swearer, 1995), demonstrates a fundamental shift in the understanding of attachment. The old way of clinging to the sweetness of life and recoiling from life's horrors reflects a delusional enmeshment with the "flimsiest of screens." The new way, the enlightened way, reveals a respectful regard for all sentient beings equally, and a sincere desire to do whatever possible to free them from their suffering. Each suffers uniquely in a suffering shared by all.

* P. 89

For each to begin to see the light, as it were, the Buddha adopted skillful means (*upaya,* in Sanskrit). So his brief return to his jewel-studded throne allowed his wife to understand that he was there for her in the way she needed, and further, that he was there for her in a way of which she had never dreamt. It was said that the Buddha's skillful means were transcendent: He could say "Ah," and each listener would hear the sermon each most needed to hear.

In that fabled capacity deeply to know and address the other's state of mind, the Buddha demonstrates what psy-

* P. 91

choanalysis describes as "mentalization": the capacity to surmise another's—as well as one's own—mental states. The capacity develops through secure attachment, in the sense that the mother is able "to contain the [distressed] baby and respond, in terms of physical care, in a manner that shows awareness of the child's mental state yet reflect coping . . ." (Fonagy, 2001, p. 166). The Cartesian problem of how to know another's mind is solved through the experience of being known.

Being known by you permits my knowing you. As well, being known by you permits my knowing you as I know myself, as a self. Knowing, however, can constrain and objectify mental states revealed on closer introspection to be ever-changing and elusive. Truly secure attachment becomes, from a Buddhist point of view, a capacity for non-attachment, i.e., a capacity fully to experience mental states without becoming stuck in them. I know who I am securely enough to permit the insecurity of letting myself go. We can guess, but cannot know, what's next. We place

* P. 91

each other as evolving, knowing entities, acting and reacting and interacting consciously in the stories of our lives.

Psychoanalysis elicits the telling of those stories (Spence, 1982; Schafer, 1992). The disjunction between my story as I tell it and my story as you retell it fractures my story, demands revision. Pirandello (1926) tells the story of a man driven mad by the realization that his self could never be known by another, and that he could never know the self another took him to be. Yet there are degrees of knowing. The psychoanalytic situation proffers a way to tell one's story more authentically, until the centrality of one's separateness dissolves.

* P. 92
The analogy to fiction is productive. In an effort to clarify what makes an author's work distinctively her or his own, the critic Michael Wood (1995) suggests a contrast between style and signature. Style as a manner of writing is distinctive yet not necessarily unique. A skilled imitator can adopt another author's style, and perhaps pass off as authentic a story not truly that other author's own. Signature, by contrast, though perhaps more elusive because never the same signature twice, is at base inimitably, authentically unique. Signature marks the story as the real thing.

Might my signature way of being endure? Borges (2000), I surmise, would suggest otherwise. He, along with Ralph Waldo Emerson, suspects an even subtler "universal author," a signatory of all signatures, the writer of writers. Such transcendental unity in seeming multiplicity lends itself, I think, to a Buddhist worldview where forms come empty.

In the end, at the subtlest level, signature is neither mine nor yours, but an aspect of what occurs. My signature self is a product of the moment wherein everything exists all at once, interconnected and interdependent and inter-sustaining. Me-here and you-there is one aspect of that larger whole where everything is here and inter-
* P. 94
locked, arising and re-becoming all at once. We co-create all at once, like "limbs and members of a living whole" (Shantideva, seventh century C.E., v.114; 1997, p. 126).

We are attached, like it or not. So the stories we create matter not just to ourselves. We can create the dog-eat-dog

* P. 94

world of Thomas Hobbes (1651), where life is "brutish and short." Or we can notice in a strawberry the allure of the moment, the choice-point it poses (per the story told by Joseph Goldstein, 1983; recounted by Stuart Pizer, 2003, p. 149). We are faced with one another. I cannot reduce you to a character in my story. You are more than I can know.

* P. 95

Our confrontation with one another demands from each of us an ethical response, which is the opening of our being to otherness through letting go the isolate self one presumes one knows. No clinging. "The ethical relation arises when those who have ears to hear hear the voice of the other—the widow, the orphan and the stranger . . . a voice that is summoning them, calling them into question, even accusing them. Far from being at the center and in charge, I now find myself in the dock" (Westphal, 2003, p. 35, describing the philosophical position of Emmanuel Levinas; Levinas, 1999). Hickory, dickory, dock.

OUR LOVE

empty

CHAPTER 6. MEMORIES, DREAMS, PERCEPTIONS

*P. 103

The intentional construction of "palaces of memory" is a time-honored mnemonic device (Johnson, 1991, pp. xiii–xiv) whereby with practice one builds in mind a palace of rooms. The placement of every item in every room is an associational trigger to a memory. The diligent palace-builder can thereby recall long lists of facts and dates and names ever impressive to the uninitiated. Such a palace is a conscious construction. Neurologically, one's world is the conscious projection of an unconscious construction.

The Buddhist sutras are themselves a kind of palace of memory. Long passed down in the oral tradition of recita-

*P. 104
*P. 104

tion, their doorway is the formulaic "Thus I am told."

Palaces can be prisons. Remembering to forget (Langan, 1997) affords an escape from the palace where one might wander endlessly lost. The Diamond Sutra (Mu

*P. 105
*P. 105

Soeng, 2000) is a re-minder, a recalibrator of reality: nothing to remember, nothing to forget. Having forgotten how to forget (Phillips, 1994; see *P. 46 for quota-

*P. 105

tion) guarantees entrapment. You wake to find yourself "thrown" (Binswanger, 1963, following Heidegger) into a world you did not create, until and unless with luck you come across a reminder, a puzzling key to the locked palace door, revealing it to be your creation after all. Only no palace is also no you. All palaces crumble.

Do I react to that crumbling with a frenzy of attempted

*P. 106

maintenance? Erich Fromm's (1976) *To Have or To Be?* critiqued American society for its frenzied effort to have more and more while managing simply to be less and less. One is trapped, for example, in having sex, not knowing how to make love. Experience becomes a commodity: been there, done that. The doing, to my mind, is what can

*P. 106

obscure the being. The poet Yeats said it: "things fall apart/

the center cannot hold." Doing begets doing, while all palaces crumble. Being stays.

The psychoanalyst Emmanuel Ghent once asked me to respond to his work for part of a book that was never completed. He had written a paper on psychological surrender (Ghent, 1990) to which I often return. He wrote of surrender not as a defeat, a giving up, but rather as a release, letting oneself go into unknown possibilities. I

* P. 106

don't know if it was really a surrender, but up came the memory of my walk across the crumbling scree. The walking was doing, but that time, I think, doing touched being,

* P. 107

surrendered to the moment (Ghent, 1990; Weber, 2003; Csikszentmihalyi, 1997).

The problem with doing is its voracious and headlong automaticity. More and more, over and over, it just keeps

* P. 107
* P. 108

doing. "Deautomitization" (Deikman, 1966) stops the mentational doing. Apperception need not occlude perception. Being may moreso be unobscured.

* P. 108
* P. 108

How? Perhaps Bromberg's (1998) standing in the spaces, like Phillips's (1994) remembering to forget, describes a mental posture that can glimpse the mystical

* P. 109

ground of being. The anonymous hermit monk (Way, 1986) found it seven centuries ago not in the English midlands where he lived but between his clouds of forgetting

* P. 109

and unknowing. Borges (1949) describes it in a story as the "aleph," a point containing all points, all moments of time, visible if one lies in the proper place and squints at the proper angle (described in Langan, 2003a, p. 141). The

* P. 109
* P. 109
* P. 110

monk thought it God, and "He is your being" (Way, 1986, pp. 113–114). The other English monk, Ajahn Sucitto (2002), finds it no farther away than here, verily now. Nothing need be done. The Venerable Lama Gendun Rinpoche (Gendun, 1995; thanks to Larry Rosenberg for drawing it to attention) sings:

Happiness cannot be found
through great effort and willpower,
but is already present, in open relaxation
And letting go.
Don't strain yourself:
there is nothing to do or undo . . .
Nothing to do or undo,
Nothing to force,
nothing to want
and nothing missing—
Emaho! Marvelous!
Everything happens by itself.

Yet for everything to happen by itself, I must surrender.

* P. 111 To take the tantric turn of Tibetan Buddhism (Blofeld, 1970; Chögyam, 1995; Gehlek, 2001), becoming one with the object of contemplation, I must let go of myself The surrender is extreme: I die to rise anew not as the object, but as the subject of contemplation. Paradoxically, the mental posture is not an assiduous doing, but an assiduous holding to undoing, which holding is no doing in itself.

I think of the Greek myth of the sea god, Proteus (Langan, 1997b). To win his homeward wind, the becalmed Menelaos must seize the shape-shifting god and not let go. Proteus "becomes a clawing lion, the strangling coils of a writhing snake, the furied charge of a gnashing boar, then drowning wall of raging water and crushing fall of towering tree" (p. 46). How can these things be held? * P. 111 They cannot. Menelaos succeeds through holding to holding itself.

In the psychoanalytic situation, too, there is a holding to holding. Each party begins with a version of reality, and tries, in a sense, to inflict it on the other. The unconscious * P. 112 struggle between analyst and analysand requires a mutual

elasticity (Ferenczi, 1928) so that through the interactive
push and pull between them, realities can change. What

* P. 112
was held so dearly opens to what had been unformulated

* P. 112
(Stern, 1997), unthought (Bollas, 1992), dissociated

* P. 112
(Bromberg, 1998). This can only happen when beneath
the holding to one or the other reality, there is also a holding to the psychoanalytic endeavor of unholding those suf-
focating realities the better to become.

With the thread of attention we stitch together self-
states, realms of inner experience. We dangle between
subjectivities, holding the thread to find a way, each of us

* P. 113
imagination embodied (as described for the dreamer
Berthe by Robert Bosnak, 2003, pp. 685–686). And
most importantly, we loop our threads round one
another, since "'life' is the experience of our connection

* P. 114
with the rest of humanity"(Bromberg, 2003b, p. 704).

* P. 114
We live in and through our affiliations with one another
(Langan, 2003a).

In myself, I am nothing. Shakespeare (1623) reminds us,

* P. 114
"Nor I, nor any man that but man is, / With nothing shall be
pleased till he be eased/ With being nothing"(Richard II,
V.5.31–41). "Eased with being nothing" describes empti-

* P. 115
ness. We are empty. We share with the Buddha ("One Who
Has Gone Beyond") and with each and every being that
same transcendent capacity, findable, fully present: a
Buddha within (Lopez, 1995, p. 23).

* P. 116
So here we are, all together, interdependent on one
another to live (Nhat Hanh, 2002). We fill each other's
heads with thoughts, our bodies with food, our world
with comforts and meanings and purpose and doings, taking care of one another. We find, if we stop to notice, if we
pause to be, the spacious freedom of being empty still.

Parting

This last conversation between the analyst and the analysand plumbs undercurrents of what on the surface is essentially a positive relationship. They do esteem one another and are careful to convey and protect that positive regard. Yet at another level and at the same time, each ruthlessly (Winnicott, 1971) uses the other for his own ends: to preserve the security of a known role in relation to one another, to harbor fantasies of superiority or greater power, to avoid overwhelming shame and doubt.

* P. 117

Their relationship is, indeed, like the raft in Twain's (1884) *Huckleberry Finn*. It is shared and cared for by both, and carries them in relative safety over the deeper ambivalencies, rages, and fears that can overturn relationship. Their raft floats.

They allow each other room to be. The analyst literally takes the analysand into his room; in the end, the analysand provides a mental room for the analyst. Providing room or psychological space for the other to be otherwise arises from generosity towards the other. Instead of holding the other person in a headlock of how that other person must be (to preserve one's own headlock belief as to who one is and how), generosity permits openness to change. When the analysand associates to

* P. 120

the title of Arthur Kopit's (1960) absurdist play, *Oh Dad, Poor Dad, Mama's Hung You in the Closet and I'm Feeling So Sad,* he misremembers the title, substituting "dear" for "poor" dad. "Poor" would consign dad to the bad-guy role he has so long occupied. "Dear" more generously allows difference.

* P. 120

Likewise, "being dismissive or being merged" as ways of living both reflect, in Buddhist terms, clinging, an ungenerous grasping. The merging is a kind of greed, the dismissiveness a kind of aversion, and both the greed and the aversion avoid the more generous option of letting go, allowing otherness, surrendering to impermanence and emptiness.

A similar letting go is required of you, the reader, and me, the author, while the analysand leaves, the analyst fades to emptiness, and the book ends. As we watch, in mind's eye, the analyst's eyes half close, let us allow to cross his mind, as must cross our mind borne by these very words, the plaintive query (and koan) of Johnny Mercer (1938), "Jeepers, creepers, where'd you get those peepers?/Jeepers, creepers, where'd you get those eyes?" I find an answer on a scrap of paper in my pocket: "Learn where is wisdom, where is strength, where is understanding,/That thou mayest also know length of days and life,/The source of the light in the eyes and peace."

* P. 122

References

(Bookshelves)

Abbott, E.A. (1884), *Flatland: A Romance of Many Dimensions*. New York: Dover, 1952.

Agee, J. (1957), *A Death in the Family*. New York: McDowell, Obolensky.

Alford, C.F. (2002), *Levinas, the Frankfurt School and Psychoanalysis*. Middletown, Connecticut: Wesleyan University Press.

Armstrong, K. (1993), *A History of God: The 4000-Year Quest of Judaism, Christianity and Islam*. New York: Ballantine Books.

Armstrong, K. (2001), *Buddha*. New York: Viking Penguin.

Aron, L. (1996), *A Meeting of Minds: Mutuality in Psychoanalysis*. Hillsdale, New Jersey: Analytic Press.

Batchelor, S. (1983), *Alone with Others: An Existential Approach to Buddhism*. Foreword by J. Blofeld. New York: Grove Press.

Benjamin, J. (1988), *The Bonds of Love: Psychoanalysis, Feminism, and the Problem of Domination*. New York: Pantheon Books.

Binswanger, L. (1963), *Being-in-the-World*. Trans. J. Needleman. New York: Basic Books.

Blechner, M.J. (2001), *The Dream Frontier*. Hillsdale, New Jersey: Analytic Press.

Blofeld, J. (1970), *The Tantric Mysticism of Tibet: A Practical Guide*. New York: Causeway Books, 1974.

Bobrow, J. (2003), "Moments of Truth—Truths of the Moment" in Safran, J.D., ed. (2003), *op.cit.*

Bollas, C. (1992), *Being a Character: Psychoanalysis and Self Experience*. New York: Hill and Wang.

Borges, J.L. (1949), "The Aleph," trans. A. Hurley, in *Jorge Luis Borges: Collected Fictions*. New York: Viking, 1998.

Borges, J.L. (1969), "Cambridge," trans. H. Rogers, from *In Praise of Darkness* in *Jorge Luis Borges: Selected Poems.* Ed. A. Coleman. New York: Viking Penguin, 1999.

Borges, J.L. (2000), *This Craft of Verse.* Ed. C-A. Mihailescu. Cambridge, Massachusetts: Harvard University Press.

Bosnak, R. (1996), *Tracks in the Wilderness of Dreaming: Exploring Interior Landscape through Practical Dreamwork.* New York: Delacorte Press.

Bosnak, R. (2003), "Embodied Imagination" in *Contemporary Psychoanalysis,* **39**#4:683–696.

Bromberg, P.M. (1998), *Standing in the Spaces: Essays on Clinical Process, Trauma, and Dissociation.* Hillsdale, New Jersey: Analytic Press.

Bromberg, P.M. (2003a), Personal communication 19 April 2003.

Bromberg, P.M. (2003b), "On Being One's Dream: Some Reflections on Robert Bosnak's 'Embodied Imagination'" in *Contemporary Psychoanalysis,* **39**#4:697–710.

Buber, M. (1923), *I and Thou.* Trans. W. Kaufman. New York: Charles Scribner's Sons, 1970.

Chang, G.C.C., ed. & trans. (1977), *The Hundred Thousand Songs of Milarepa.* Vols. I & II. Boston: Shambhala.

Chögyam, N. (1995), *Wearing the Body of Visions.* New York: Aro Books.

Clark, C. & Holquist, M. (1984), *Mikhail Bakhtin.* Cambridge, Massachusetts: Harvard University Press.

Coleridge, S.T. (1817), *Biographia Literaria: Or, Biographical Sketches of My Literary Life and Opinions.* Eds., J. Engell & W.J. Bate. Princeton: Bollingen Foundation, Princeton University Press, 1983.

Coles, R. (1990), *The Spiritual Life of Children.* Boston: Houghton Mifflin.

Csikszentmihalyi, M. (1997), *Finding Flow: The Psychology of Engagement with Everyday Life.* New York: Basic Books.

Deikman, J.A. (1966), "Deautomitization and the Mystic Experience" in Tart, C.T., ed., (1972), *Altered States of Consciousness.* New York: Wiley.

Dennett, D. (1991), *Consciousness Explained.* Boston: Little, Brown.

Descartes, R. (1637), *Discourse on Method and the Meditations.* Trans. F.E. Sutcliffe. New York and London: Penguin, 1968.

De Silva, L.A. (1979). *The Problem of the Self in Buddhism and Christianity.* Ed. J. Hick. New York: Harper & Row.

Edelman, G.M. (2004), *Wider Than the Sky: The Phenomenal Gift of Consciousness.* New Haven: Yale University Press.

Edelman, G.M. & Tononi, G. (2000), *A Universe of Consciousness: How Matter Becomes Imagination.* New York: Basic Books.

Eigen, M. (1993), *The Electrified Tightrope.* Ed., A. Phillips. Northvale, New Jersey: Jason Aronson.

Eigen, M. (2001), *Ecstasy.* Middletown, Connecticut: Wesleyan University Press.

Engler, J. (2004), Unpublished talk on Buddhism and psychoanalysis at the invitation of the New York University Postdoctoral Program in Psychotherapy and Psychoanalysis, 9 April 2004.

Epstein, M. (1995), *Thoughts without a Thinker: Psychotherapy from a Buddhist Perspective.* New York: Basic Books.

Erikson, E.H. (1963), *Childhood and Society.* 2nd edition. New York: W.W. Norton.

Erikson, E.H. (1969), *Gandhi's Truth: On the Origins of Militant Nonviolence.* New York: W.W. Norton.

Fairbairn, W.R.D. (1958), "On the Nature and Aims of Psycho-Analytical Treatment" in the *International Journal of Psycho-Analysis,* **39**:374–385.

Farber, L.H. (1966), *The Ways of the Will.* New York: Basic Books.

Fenton, J. (2003), "Turgenev's Banana" in the *New York Review of Books,* L#2. Includes a review of Alphonse Daudet's *In the Land of Pain,* ed. & trans. J. Barnes. New York: Knopf.

Ferenczi, S. (1928), "The Elasticity of Psycho-Analytic Technique." In *Final Contributions to the Problems and Methods of Psycho-Analysis.* London: Hogarth Press, 1955.

Flye, J.H. (1971), *Letters of James Agee to Father Flye.* 2nd edition. Boston: Houghton Mifflin.

Fonagy, P. (2001), *Attachment Theory and Psychoanalysis.* New York: Other Press.

Freud, S. (1900), *The Interpretation of Dreams.* In *The Standard Edition of the Complete Psychological Works of Sigmund Freud, Vol. IV.* London: Hogarth Press, 1953.

Freud, S. (1912), "Recommendations to Physicians Practising Psycho-Analysis." *Standard Edition,* XII:111–112. London: Hogarth Press.

Freud, S. (1923), "Two Encyclopædia Articles." *Standard Edition,* XVIII:235–262. London: Hogarth Press, 1958.

Fromm, E. (1941), *Escape from Freedom.* New York: Farrar & Rinehart.

Fromm, E. (1976), *To Have or To Be?* New York: Harper & Row.

Gehlek, N. (2001), *Good Life, Good Death: Tibetan Wisdom on Reincarnation.* New York: Riverhead Books.

Gehlek, N. (2003), *Jewel Heart Prayers.* Ann Arbor, Michigan: Jewel Heart.

Gendun (1995), "Free and Easy: A Spontaneous Vajra Song" in N. Khenpo, *Natural Great Perfection: Dzogchen Teaching and Vajra Songs.* Trans. S. Das. Ithaca, New York: Snow Lion Publications.

Gergen, K. (1985), *The Saturated Self: Dilemmas of Identity in Contemporary Life.* New York: Basic Books.

Ghent, E. (1990), "Masochism, Submission, Surrender: Masochism as a Perversion of Surrender" in *Contemporary Psychoanalysis,* **26**#1: 108–136.

Ghent, E. (2002), "Wish, Need, Drive: Motive in Light of Dynamic Systems Theory and Edelman's Selectionist Theory" in *Psychoanalytic Dialogues,* **12**#5:763–808.

Goldstein, J. (1983), "Bare Attention." Talk delivered at the Insight Meditation Society, Barre, Massachusetts, May 27.

Goldstein, J., and Kornfield, J. (1987), *Seeking the Heart of Wisdom: The Path of Insight Meditation.* Boston: Shambhala.

Goleman, D. (2003), *Destructive Emotions: How Can We Overcome Them? A Scientific Dialogue with the Dalai Lama.* New York: Bantam Books.

Govinda, A. (1960), *Foundations of Tibetan Mysticism According to the Teachings of the Great Mantra* OM MANI PADME HUM. New York: Samuel Weiser, 1970.

Govinda, A. (1970), *The Way of the White Clouds.* Boulder: Shambhala.

Greenberg, J.R. & Mitchell, S.A. (1983), *Object Relations in Psychoanalytic Theory.* Cambridge, Massachusetts: Harvard University Press.

Greenberg, J.R. (1991), *Œdipus and Beyond: A Clinical Theory.* Cambridge, Massachusetts: Harvard University Press.

Greene, B. (1999), *The Elegant Universe: Superstrings, Hidden Dimensions, and the Quest for the Ultimate Theory.* New York: W.W. Norton.

Gyatso, T. (2001), *Stages of Meditation.* Trans. L. Jordhen, L.C. Ganchenpa, J. Russell. Ithaca, New York: Snow Lion Publications.

Gyatso, T. (2002), *Essence of the Heart Sutra: The Dalai Lama's Heart of Wisdom Teachings.* Trans. & ed. by G.T. Jinpa. Boston: Wisdom Publications.

Gyatso, T. and Sheng-yen (1999), *Meeting of Minds: A Dialogue on Tibetan and Chinese Buddhism.* New York: Dharma Drum Publications.

Hampshire, S. (1993), "The Last Charmer" in the *New York Review of Books,* XL#5:15–18. Reviewed are Furbank, P.N., *Diderot: A Critical Biography,*

New York: Knopf; and Furbank, P.N., ed. & trans., *'This Is Not A Story'* *and Other Stories by Denis Diderot,* University of Missouri Press.

Harris, A. (2005), *Gender as Soft Assembly.* Hillsdale, New Jersey: Analytic Press.

Hawking, S.W. (1988), *A Brief History of Time: From the Big Bang to Black Holes.* New York: Bantam Books.

Hawking, S.W. (2001), *The Universe in a Nutshell.* New York: Bantam Books.

Hobbes, T. (1651), *Leviathan.* Ed. C.B. Macpherson. London: Penguin, 1985.

Hoffman, I.Z. (1998), *Ritual and Spontaneity in the Psychoanalytic Process: A Dialectical-Constructivist View.* Hillsdale, New Jersey: Analytic Press.

Hume, D. (1739) *A Treatise on Human Nature: Being an Attempt to Introduce the Experimental Method of Reasoning into Moral Subjects.* Ed. E.C. Mossner. London and New York: Penguin, 1984.

Hunt, H.T. (1995), *On the Nature of Consciousness.* New Haven: Yale University Press.

James, W. (1902), *The Varieties of Religious Experience: A Study in Human Nature, being the Gifford Lectures on Natural Religion delivered at Edinburgh in 1901–1902.* New York: Library of America, 1987.

Johnson, G. (1991), *In the Palaces of Memory: How We Build the Worlds Inside Our Heads.* New York: Knopf.

Jones, J.W. (1991), *Contemporary Psychoanalysis and Religion: Transference and Transcendence.* New Haven: Yale University Press.

Jones, J.W. (2002), *Terror and Transformation: The Ambiguity of Religion in Psychoanalytic Perspective.* New York: Brunner-Routledge.

Jung, C.G. (1961), *Memories, Dreams, Reflections.* Ed. A. Jaffé; trans. R. & C. Winston. New York: Vintage Books.

Kalu, K.D.C. (1986), *The Dharma That Illuminates All Beings Like the Light of the Sun and the Moon.* Trans. J. Gyatso; ed. Kagyu Thubten Choling Translation Committee. Albany: State University of New York Press.

Kopit, A. (1960), *Oh Dad, Poor Dad, Mama's Hung You in the Closet and I'm Feeling So Sad: A Pseudoclassical Tragifarce in a Bastard French Tradition.* New York: Samuel French.

Langan, R.P. (1993), "The Depth of the Field" in *Contemporary Psychoanalysis,* **29**#4:628–644.

Langan, R.P. (1995), "I Thou Other: Fluid Being in Triadic Context" in *Contemporary Psychoanalysis,* **31**#2:327–339.

Langan, R.P. (1997a), "On Free-Floating Attention" in *Psychoanalytic Dialogues,* **7**#6:819–839.

Langan, R.P. (1997b), "Proteus Reprised" in *International Forum of Psychoanalysis,* **6**#1:45–49.

Langan, R.P. (1999a), "Coming to Be: Change by Affiliation" in *Contemporary Psychoanalysis,* **35**#1:67–80.

Langan, R.P. (1999b), "What on Closer Examination Disappears" in *American Journal of Psychoanalysis,* **59**#1:87–96.

Langan, R.P. (2000), "Someplace in Mind" in *International Forum of Psychoanalysis,* **9**#1–2:69–75.

Langan, R.P. (2003a), "The Dissolving of Dissolving Itself," in Safran, J.D., ed. (2003), *op.cit.*

Langan, R.P. (2003b), "A Saturated Solution," in Safran, J.D., ed. (2003), *op.cit.*

Levenson, E.A. (1972), *The Fallacy of Understanding: An Inquiry into the Changing Structure of Psychoanalysis.* New York: Basic Books.

Levenson, E.A. (1983), *The Ambiguity of Change: An Inquiry into the Nature of Psychoanalytic Reality.* New York: Basic Books.

Levinas, E. (1999), *Alterity and Transcendence.* Trans. M.B. Smith. New York: Columbia University Press.

Lopez, D.S., ed. (1995), *Buddhism in Practice.* Princeton, New Jersey: Princeton University Press.

Lopez, D.S., ed. (1997), *Religions of Tibet in Practice.* Princeton, New Jersey: Princeton University Press.

Mandelbrot, B.B. (1983), *The Fractal Geometry of Nature.* New York: W.H. Freeman.

Matthiessen, P. (1978), *The Snow Leopard.* New York: Penguin Books, 1996.

May, R., Angel, E., Ellenberger, H.F., eds. (1958), *Existence: A New Dimension in Psychiatry and Psychology.* New York: Basic Books.

Mendis, K.N.G. (1979), *On the No-Self Characteristic (Anatta-Lakkhana Sutta).* Kandy, Sri Lanka: Buddhist Publication Society.

Mercer, J. (1938), "Jeepers Creepers." Lyrics by J. Mercer; Music by H. Warren. First released as sung to a horse by Louis Armstrong in the movie, *Going Places.* Hollywood: Warner Brothers.

Mitchell, S.A. (1988), *Relational Concepts in Psychoanalysis: An Integration.* Cambridge, Massachusetts: Harvard University Press.

Mitchell, S.A. (2000), *Relationality: From Attachment to Intersubjectivity.* Hillsdale, New Jersey: Analytic Press.

Molino, A., ed. (1998), *The Couch and the Tree: Dialogues in Psychoanalysis and Buddhism*. New York: North Point Press.

Mu Soeng (1991), *Heart Sutra: Ancient Buddhist Wisdom in the Light of Quantum Reality*. Cumberland, Rhode Island: Primary Point Press.

Mu Soeng, ed. & trans. (2000), *The Diamond Sutra: Transforming the Way We Perceive the World*. Boston: Wisdom Publications.

Nasr, S.H. (2003), "In the Beginning of Creation Was Consciousness" in *Harvard Divinity Bulletin*, **32**#1:13–16,43.

Nhat Hanh, T. (2002), *No Death, No Fear: Comforting Wisdom for Life*. New York: Riverhead Books.

Norbu, C.N. (2002), *Dream Yoga and the Practice of Natural Light*. Ed. M. Katz. Ithaca, New York: Snow Lion Publications.

Nyanoponika, T. (1949), *Abhidhamma Studies: Buddhist Explorations of Consciousness and Time*. Ed. B. Bodhi. Boston: Wisdom Publications, 1998.

Oberhelman, S.M. (1991), *The Oneirocriticon of Achmet: A Medieval Greek and Arabic Treatise on the Interpretation of Dreams*. Lubbock, Texas: Texas Tech University Press.

Obeyesekere, G. (2004), "The Buddhist Meditative Askesis: A Variety of the Visionary Experience. Excerpts from the William James Lecture for 2003–04" in the *Harvard Divinity Bulletin*, **32**#3:7–10.

Ogden, T. (1994), *Subjects of Analysis*. Northvale, New Jersey: Jason Aronson.

Olendzki, A. (2002), "The Fourth Foundation of Mindfulness" in *Insight Journal*, **19**:13–17.

Olendzki, A. (2004a), "The Fourth Foundation of Mindfulness" in *Insight Journal*, **22**:13–17.

Olendzki, A. (2004b), "A Comprehensive Matrix of Constructed Experience" in *Insight Journal*, **23**:16–17.

Paul, R.A. (1982), *The Tibetan Symbolic World: Psychoanalytic Explorations*. Chicago: University of Chicago Press.

Phillips, A. (1993), *On Kissing, Tickling and Being Bored: Psychoanalytic Essays on the Unexamined Life*. Cambridge, Massachusetts: Harvard University Press.

Phillips, A. (1994), *On Flirtation*. Cambridge, Massachusetts: Harvard University Press.

Piers, C. (2000), "Character as Self-Organizing Complexity" in *Psychoanalysis and Contemporary Thought*, **23**#1:3–34.

Pirandello, L. (1926), *One, No One, and One Hundred Thousand*. Trans. W. Weaver. Boston: Eridanos Press, 1990.

Pizer, S.A. (1998), *Building Bridges: The Negotiation of Paradox in Psychoanalysis.* Hillsdale, New Jersey: Analytic Press.

Pizer, S.A. (2003), "Imagining Langan: A Transcendence of Self." Commentary in Safran, J.D. (2003), *op.cit.*

Rapaport, D., trans. & ed. (1951), *Organization and Pathology of Thought: Selected Sources.* New York: Columbia University Press.

Rosenberg, L. (1998), *Breath by Breath: The Liberating Practice of Insight Meditation.* Boston: Shambhala.

Safran, J.D., ed. (2003), *Psychoanalysis and Buddhism: An Unfolding Dialogue.* Boston: Wisdom Publications.

Schafer, R. (1983), *The Analytic Attitude.* New York: Basic Books.

Schafer, R. (1992), *Retelling a Life: Narration and Dialogue in Psychoanalysis.* New York: Basic Books.

Searle, J. (1992), *The Rediscovery of the Mind.* Cambridge, Massachusetts: MIT Press.

Segall, S.R., ed. (2003), *Encountering Buddhism: Western Psychology and Buddhist Teachings.* Albany: State University of New York Press.

Shakespeare, W. (1623), *The Tragedy of King Richard the Second.* Ed. R.T. Petersson. New Haven: Yale University Press, 1957.

Shantideva (1997), *The Way of the Bodhisattva: A Translation of the Bodhicharyavatara.* Trans. Padmakara Translation Group. Boston: Shambhala.

Silberer, H. (1909), "Report on a Method of Eliciting and Observing Certain Symbolic Hallucination-Phenomena" in Rapaport (1951), *op.cit.*, pp. 195–207.

Silberer, H. (1912), "On Symbol Formation" in Rapaport (1951), *op.cit.*, pp. 208–233.

Sircar, R. (1999), *The Psycho-Ethical Aspects of Abhidhamma.* Lanham, Maryland: University Press of America.

Spence, D. (1982), *Narrative Truth and Historical Truth: Meaning and Interpretation in Psychoanalysis.* New York: W.W. Norton.

Spezzano, C. & Gargiulo, G.J., eds. (1997), *Soul on the Couch: Spirituality, Religion and Morality in Contemporary Psychoanalysis.* Hillsdale, New Jersey: Analytic Press.

Stern, D.B. (1997), *Unformulated Experience: From Dissociation to Imagination in Psychoanalysis.* Hillsdale, New Jersey: Analytic Press.

Strand, M. (1964), "Keeping Things Whole." In Strand (1998), *op.cit.*, p. 10.

Strand, M. (1978), "For Jessica, My Daughter." In Strand (1998), *op.cit.*, p. 120.

Strand, M. (1998), *Selected Poems*. New York: Knopf.

Sucitto, A. (2001), "A Ripple in a Pond: An Interview with Ajahn Sucitto" in *Insight,* newsletter of the Insight Meditation Society and the Barre Center for Buddhist Studies, Barre, Massachusetts.

Sucitto, A. (2002), "Aimless Wandering." Talk at the Insight Meditation Society, Barre, Massachusetts, April 25.

Suler, J.R. (1993), *Contemporary Psychoanalysis and Eastern Thought*. Albany: State University of New York Press.

Sullivan, H.S. (1953), *The Interpersonal Theory of Psychiatry.* Eds. H.S. Perry & M.L. Gawel. New York: W.W. Norton.

Swearer, D.K. (1995), "Bimba's Lament." Ch. 43 pp. 541–552 in Lopez, D.S. (1995), *op.cit.*

Thurman, R.A.F., ed. & trans. (1994), THE TIBETAN BOOK OF THE DEAD *as popularly known in the West, Known in Tibet as the* THE GREAT BOOK OF NATURAL LIBERATION THROUGH UNDERSTANDING IN THE BETWEEN, *Composed by Padma Sambhava, Discovered by Karma Lingpa*. New York: Bantam Books.

Thurman, R.A.F. (1996), *Essential Tibetan Buddhism*. San Francisco: HarperSanFrancisco.

Trungpa, C. (1969), *Meditation in Action*. Berkeley: Shambhala.

Twain, M. (1884), *The Adventures of Huckleberry Finn (Tom Sawyer's Comrade)*. New York: Harper and Brothers, 1923.

Varela, F.J., ed. (1997), *Sleeping, Dreaming, and Dying: An Exploration of Consciousness with the Dalai Lama*. Boston: Wisdom Publications.

Walker, J. (18—), Memorial bust inscription of James Walker. Memorial Hall, Harvard University, Cambridge, Massachusetts.

Way, R., trans. (1986), *The Cloud of Unknowing and the Letter of Private Direction*. Wheathampstead, Hertfordshire, England: Anthony Clarke.

Weber, S.L. (2003), "An Analyst's Surrender." In Safran, J.D., ed. (2003), *op.cit.*

Weber, S.L. (2004), "Doubt, Arrogance and Humility," discussion of J. Safran, "Before the Ass Has Gone the Horse Has Already Come," both talks given at the invitation of the Psychoanalytic Psychotherapy Study Center, New York City, 13 November 2004. Joint publication pending in *Contemporary Psychoanalysis*.

Weiss, J., Samson, H., and the Mt. Zion Psychotherapy Research Group (1986), *The Psychoanalytic Process: Theory, Clinical Observation, and Empirical Research*. New York: Guilford.

Westphal, M. (2003), "Blind Spots: Christianity and Postmodern Philoso-
    phy" in *Christian Century* (June 14, 2003), pp. 32–35.
Winnicott, D.W. (1971), *Playing and Reality.* London: Tavistock, 1986.
Wolstein, B. (1962), *Irrational Despair: An Examination of Existential Analysis.*
    New York: Free Press of Glencoe, Macmillan. [See *P.77]
Wood, M. (1995), *The Magician's Doubts: Nabokov and the Risks of Fiction.*
    Princeton: Princeton University Press.

INDEX

About Wisdom Publications

Wisdom Publications, a nonprofit publisher, is dedicated to making available authentic works relating to Buddhism, for the benefit of all. We publish books by ancient and modern masters in all traditions of Buddhism, translations of important texts, and original scholarship. Additionally, we offer books that explore East-West themes unfolding as traditional Buddhism encounters our modern culture in all its aspects. Our titles are published with the appreciation of Buddhism as a living philosophy, and with the special commitment to preserve and transmit important works from Buddhism's many traditions.

To learn more about Wisdom, or to browse books online, visit our website at www.wisdompubs.org.

You may rerquest a copy of our catalog online or by writing to this address:

Wisdom Publications
199 Elm Street
Somerville, Massachusetts 02144 USA
Telephone: (617) 776-7416
Fax: (617) 776-7841
Email: info@wisdompubs.org
www.wisdompubs.org

The Wisdom Trust

As a nonprofit publisher, Wisdom is dedicated to the publication of Dharma books for the benefit of all sentient beings and dependent upon the kindness and generosity of sponsors in order to do so. If you would like to make a donation to Wisdom, you may do so through our website or our Somerville office. If you would like to help sponsor the publication of a book, please write or email us at the address above.

Thank you.

Wisdom is a nonprofit, charitable 501(c)(3) organization affiliated with the Foundation for the Preservation of the Mahayana Tradition (FPMT).